Valley of the Shadow

Jennifer Townsend

The ESV® Bible (The Holy Bible, English Standard Version®). ESV® Text Edition: 2016. Copyright © 2001 by Crossway, a publishing ministry of Good News Publishers. The ESV® text has been reproduced in cooperation with and by permission of Good News Publishers. Unauthorized reproduction of this publication is prohibited. All rights reserved.

The Holy Bible, English Standard Version (ESV) is adapted from the Revised Standard Version of the Bible, copyright Division of Christian Education of the National Council of the Churches of Christ in the U.S.A. All rights reserved.

Copyright © 2018 Jennifer Townsend

All rights reserved. No portion of this material may be reproduced or distributed without the written permission of Jennifer Townsend and/or her legal representative(s). Brief portions may be quoted for review purposes.

ISBN: 9-781723-850219

The people came up out of the Jordan on the tenth day of the first month, and they encamped at Gilgal on the east border of Jericho. And those twelve stones, which they took out of the Jordan, Joshua set up at Gilgal. And he said to the people of Israel, "When your children ask their fathers in times to come, 'What do these stones mean?' then you shall let your children know, 'Israel passed over this Jordan on dry ground.' For the LORD your God dried up the waters of the Jordan for you until you passed over, as the LORD your God did to the Red Sea, which He dried up for us until we passed over, so that all the peoples on the earth may know that the hand of the LORD is mighty, that you may fear the LORD your God forever."
~Joshua 4:19–24~

This book is the altar of my remembrance. May I never forget the kindness of my God as He graciously and patiently taught me the lessons of the valley of shadow of death.

CONTENTS

	Acknowledgments	vii
	A Word to the Reader	ix
	A Personal Valley	1
Chapter 1	Valley of the Shadow	3
Chapter 2	Praise and Thanksgiving	11
Chapter 3	Valley of Tears	19
Chapter 4	The Living Word of God	25
Chapter 5	End-of-Life Stories	37
Chapter 6	Grace and Space	47
Chapter 7	The Day-to-Day Journey	61
	Conclusion	67
	Appendix: What is a Bible-Believing Christian?	69
	Endnotes	73

ACKNOWLEDGMENTS

The gracious sacrifice of time, resources, and advice from many people made this book a reality. God assembled a wonderful team to help with this monumental task, giving me the confidence of heart and peace of mind to write without distraction.

During Thanksgiving of 2017, Brenda Henderson encouraged me to self-publish a book. Her encouragement was simple as she told me that those who knew me and knew my story would like to hear from me. She was the last in a long line of ladies who encouraged me to write. Brenda introduced me to the world of self-publishing and graciously spent much time explaining the process. Thank you, Brenda, for your encouragement and advice along the way.

My aunt, Barbara Lasoff, has worked in publishing for thirty-nine years as a development editor and as a managing editor for the Institute for Applied Systems Analysis in Laxenburg, Austria, Houghton Mifflin Company's College Division, and Wolters Kluwer Legal and Regulatory U.S. in the Legal Education Division. She is now a freelance editor. Aunt Barb and her husband, Nicholas Lasoff, have added much joy to my childhood and adult years. When I approached Aunt Barb about editing this book, she eagerly accepted. Her professional advice was invaluable. Thank you, Aunt Barb, for tirelessly giving of your time to help me through the editing process.

Three faithful friends read this book as I wrote it. They pointed out wording that needed to be tweaked and sent encouraging e-mails and texts to buoy my spirits when the writing process was slow. These friends prayed for me to have a clear mind as I worked through difficult chapters. They were my quiet iron-sharpening-iron friends (Proverbs 27:17) who held up my arms in this journey (Exodus 17:12). Thank you, Naomi Hall, Erica Krystowiak, and Jenny Muth for being my joyful cheerleaders in this undertaking.

Two godly couples and my brother helped me in the last step of the writing process. Pastor Richard and Mrs. Claudia Eckelbarger are the sweet parents of Todd's (my husband) first wife, Naomi. They walked their own valley of the shadow journey as they said good-bye to their daughter, and they have been a faithful and loving encouragement to Todd and me as we have walked our valleys. We are proud and blessed to call them Dad and Mom E. Matthew and Colleen Parker have been friends of mine for years. Their faithfulness both in full-time ministry and the secular workforce has been obvious to all who know them. With their joyful, upbeat, yet realistic outlook on life, Matt and Colleen have a remarkable ministry of encouragement to others. Keith Lewis, my brother, walked through this valley of the shadow with me. His perspective as a son, dad, and pastor put him in a unique position to grieve with and comfort our family. Keith's dedication to the exegesis of God's Word has been evident since his junior high days. These men and their faithful wives are known in their generations as men and women of God with a love for and deep understanding of God's Word that is both practical and timely. They spent hours double checking the scriptural content and wording of biblical truths before the book was sent to the printing press. With their input, I was able to rest assured that God and His Word would be honored. Thank you, Pastor and Mrs. Eckelbarger, Matt and Colleen Parker, and Keith, for the hours you spent helping me correctly apply God's Word.

Finally, my husband was the behind-the-scenes man who listened to the frustrations and joys I encountered in the writing process. Todd encouraged me to take this season of life to fulfill a life-long dream of mine—to author a book. Todd's first wife passed away in 2013. Five months before my mom died, Todd's mom passed away from a glioblastoma—the same type of brain tumor Mom had. We have talked, cried, and prayed our way through the lessons God has taught us in our valley journeys. Todd's godly perspective, encouragement, and prayers made this book possible. Thank you, Todd, for loving and caring for me so well. I am so thankful God brought you into my life.

A WORD TO THE READER

I do not know the circumstances of life that caused you to pick up this book. However, it is my hope and prayer that you will be encouraged by what you read in the following pages.

This book is written from my perspective as a Bible-believing Christian. In the Appendix you can find a brief synopsis of what that means.

A PERSONAL VALLEY

Christmas Eve 2015 forever changed my family. Debbie Lewis, sweet mom to my four siblings and me and adoring wife to my dad, was diagnosed with a brain tumor. In the days to follow, we learned that Mom had the most aggressive form of brain cancer—a glioblastoma.

One year and four weeks later, on January 22, 2017, Mom quietly went home to heaven in her sleep. She left behind a family of eighteen individuals (husband, children and spouses, and grandchildren) who loved her dearly. Each of us has walked his own unique path on this journey through the valley of the shadow of death. In the following pages, I share the lessons God taught me in my journey through this valley. Psalm 34:1-9 was my constant source of hope during the journey. This passage became my valley Psalm.

> I will bless the Lord at all times;
> His praise shall continually be in my mouth.
> My soul makes its boast in the Lord;
> let the humble hear and be glad.
> Oh, magnify the Lord with me,
> and let us exalt His name together!
> I sought the Lord, and He answered me
> and delivered me from all my fears.
> Those who look to Him are radiant,
> and their faces shall never be ashamed.
> This poor man cried, and the Lord heard him
> and saved him out of all his troubles.
> The angel of the Lord encamps
> around those who fear Him, and delivers
> them. Oh, taste and see that the Lord is good!
> Blessed is the man who takes refuge in Him!
> Oh, fear the Lord, you His saints,
> for those who fear Him have no lack!

CHAPTER 1
VALLEY OF THE SHADOW

Psalm 23

My thoughts often turned to Psalm 23 when I heard of a friend walking through death's valley. My view of this Psalm changed when God lead me through the valley of the shadow of death.

> 1 The Lord is my shepherd; I shall not want.
> 2 He makes me lie down in green pastures. He leads me beside still waters.
> 3 He restores my soul. He leads me in paths of righteousness for His name's sake.
> 4 Even though I walk through the valley of the shadow of death, I will fear no evil, for You are with me; Your rod and Your staff, they comfort me.
> 5 You prepare a table before me in the presence of my enemies; You anoint my head with oil; my cup overflows.
> 6 Surely goodness and mercy shall follow me all the days of my life, and I shall dwell in the house of the Lord forever.

In verses 1–3 and 5–6, David's serene portrayal of this path appeared idealistic and highly desirable in times of overwhelming horrors and fears. Prior to my valley journey, my soul would soar as I read those verses, and my joyful heart responded with a resounding, "Yes, Lord! Lead me beside still waters and give me goodness and mercy to brighten my day!" On Christmas Eve 2015, I found myself overwhelmed with many things, but among them was not a soaring heart or prayers of joy.

In the middle of the Psalm, I read the words *death*, *evil*, and *enemies*. These words were more suited to my experience. The middle of my valley journey was the longest and most emotionally draining of the whole experience. The middle included waiting for the next medical report, watching the effects of brain cancer rob Mom of her abilities, agonizing over the loss of dreams, grappling with the realization that life-long prayer requests were being answered with a definitive "no," and wishing with all my heart that I could escape to some faraway land and never hurt this much again. Those words in the middle of Psalm 23 struck fear into the heart of this very weak bit of dust called "Jenn."

So how could I reconcile the beautiful joys (vv. 1–3, 5–6) with the ugly horrors (v. 4–5) in death's valley? The phrase "the valley of the shadow of death" revealed a unique beauty in this heart-wrenching journey. This was a beauty I had never taken time to ponder; and one that would, in the long run, give me joy.

Valleys

A valley is in direct contrast to the mountain peaks around it. It is the low spot in the topography. The sun in the valley remains hidden by looming peaks for a large portion of the day. In the valley one's view of what is beyond the surrounding peaks is limited by the hard, rocky face of the mountains. The Christian life includes valleys. The walk through the valley of the shadow of death is a long, wearisome journey with limited light and limited views. The journey is filled with sleeplessness, tears, heartaches, moans of the spirit, and a deep sadness as one waits to see the sun again while dealing with harsh scenery day-in and day-out. But the valley holds much more than long nights and limited views. A recent visit to the Rocky Mountains of Colorado taught me that valleys also hold beauty.

Valleys are places of nourishment and rest. The spring mountain melt creates rivers to sustain life in the valley below. Flowers bloom as the sun occasionally peeks over the mountain tops, giving warmth and light. Hikers can rest in the valleys between mountain peaks. The storms that ravage the top of the mountains do not reach full force in the valley.

So it is in the Christian walk. The valley offers God's nourishment and protection. Psalm 23 speaks of the One who guides the Christian into this valley path. God's nourishment and protection of His child are abundantly clear as He brings him to gentle places (v. 1), meets his needs (v. 1), gives him rest (v. 2), fills him with peace (vv. 2, 5), refreshes his weary soul (vv. 3, 4), leads him in the right path (v. 4), disciplines him (v. 4), nourishes him in the midst of the most fearful confrontations (v. 5), and showers him with goodness and mercy (v. 6).

Valley of the Shadow

The geography analogy in Psalm 23 taught me that though my valley journey was dark and long, it was tempered from the harshest part of the storm by the surrounding mountain peaks of God's protection and nourishment. Although different from the mountain top experiences, this valley had its own beauty when I took time to observe it. The valley of the shadow of death, with its limited view and sunshine, is where God invited me to explore and ponder the beauty of His character traits and answers to prayer (see Chapter 2), His provision for grief (see Chapter 3), His all-sufficient Word (see Chapter 4), His perfect plan of a complete and joyous salvation (see Chapter 5), and His practical provisions for the long night seasons of life (see Chapters 6 and 7).

Robert Browning alludes to the valley experiences in a passage from his five-part epic poem "Paracelsus." He sees God bringing beautiful light to his ugly dark valley and "tempering" his sorrow with joy.

> God, Thou art love! I build my faith on that.
> . . .
> I know Thee who has kept my path, and made
> Light for me in the darkness, tempering sorrow
> So that it reached me like a solemn joy;
> It were too strange that I should doubt Thy love.
> ~Robert Browning, Part V: Paracelsus Attains~

As God taught me the lessons I share in this book, I began to see the importance and beauty of this valley journey. God taught me lessons I would not have learned in any other setting. However, Mr. Browning's phrase "tempering sorrow so that it reached me like a solemn joy" baffled me, and questions filled my mind. How could sorrow become joy? How could terminal cancer bring a "solemn joy"? In order to understand Mr. Browning's perspective, I had to consider the rest of the phrase "the valley of the shadow of death."

Shadows

Shadows are fascinating to children. Some children find them scary, while others are constantly trying to catch their shadow.

My husband and I have a picture of our shadows from our honeymoon. The sun behind us cast our shadows onto the red beach sand of Prince Edward Island. The sky was a stormy dark gray, and the sun had just peeked through the rain clouds. In that moment the blue ocean water, red sand, black shadows, and yellow sun all came together to create a beautiful picture to help us remember that wonderful experience. The shadow in that picture is only a silhouette of us. Although the viewer can see a height difference, helping him to gather some information, he cannot guess hair color, personality, the occasion of the picture, or our ages by simply looking at the shadow. A shadow indicates the form or the presence of the real thing, but it is not the actual thing. I love the verse in the middle of Psalm 23 where David stated that death for the believer is a shadow.

> Even though I walk through the valley of the shadow
> of death I will fear no evil for You are with me.
> ~Psalm 23:4~

According to this verse, Mom did not experience the entirety of death. Instead she experienced a "shadow of death." The shadow was the indication that death was near, yet death in its fullness never touched her. To fully grasp this concept of "the shadow of death," I needed to define death as the Bible defines it.

Death Defined

In the first few chapters of the Bible, we find God's definition of death. In Genesis 2 Adam was given a command along with a consequence for disobedience attached to it.

> But of the tree of knowledge of good and evil you shall
> not eat, for in the day that you eat of it you shall surely die.
> ~Genesis 2:17~

I have wondered about the statement "in the day you eat of it you shall surely die." Adam did not physically die as soon as he ate the fruit, so death, by God's definition, had to be more than just a physical state. In the moment he sinned, Adam's friendship with God changed drastically. His sin separated him spiritually from fellowship with God, and he hid from God's presence out of fear (Genesis 3:8). Adam's sin also separated him physically from God. He and Eve would be driven from God's physical presence because God's holiness could not dwell with sin (Genesis 3:23–24, Isaiah 59:2), and Adam's years on earth were numbered (Genesis 3:22–24). According to Genesis, death was separation from God's presence. Oh, the gut-wrenching pain that must have existed for both Adam and God in those first few moments of separation.

In a recent conversation with my husband, Todd reminded me that death grieves God. It wasn't supposed to be this way. Physical and spiritual death was not part of God's perfect setting for His children. In the Garden of Eden, mankind lived in the presence of God and other humans, experiencing unhindered friendship with both. Sin ruined these relationships, and great pain and suffering were the result.

Some would argue that a good God would not allow death, pain, or suffering. It was, in fact, mankind who allowed death by choosing sin. Physical and spiritual death is the consequence of sin, yet death only magnifies God's incredible goodness to undeserving mankind.

God's Goodness Revealed

For believers, how amazing it is that our good God would orchestrate the consequence for sin (death) to be the vehicle that brings us back to the original purpose of life—to be in the presence of God experiencing unhindered spiritual and physical fellowship with Him! Thus the homecoming of His child is also precious in God's eyes as He restores the perfect, original state of His creation to its intended place in His presence (Psalm 116:15).

Mom experienced only the shadow of death, not the fullness of death. Her sin, which had spiritually separated her from God, had been dealt with by Jesus's death and resurrection. On the day of her salvation, Mom's spiritual separation from God was over. When Mom took her last breath on earth, her physical separation from God was over. Only a good God could turn the punishment for Mom's sin (death) into her greatest reward and joy and the very thing for which she was created—a personal relationship with God forever in His presence. Yes, Mom only experienced a shadow of death.

David's exclamation in Psalm 34 summed up the joy that flooded my heart as I understood God's beautiful plan in the shadow of death.

> Oh, taste and see that the LORD is good!
> ~Psalm 34:8~

My heart was relieved of such a heaviness of sadness as I understood the phrase "the valley of the shadow of death." I was finally free to reflect on Mom's excited comment spoken less than a month before her death: "Jenn, have you heard where I am going?!"

The awfulness of the instrument of death (whether it be brain cancer, Alzheimer's, a car accident, or a tired old body letting go) and the human pain of saying good-bye still existed, but now I understood the "solemn joy" Mr. Browning wrote about in his poem and the joy in death Paul wrote about in 1 Corinthians 15.

> "O death, where is your victory? O death, where is your sting?" The sting of death is sin, and the power of sin is the law. But thanks be to God, who gives us the victory through our Lord Jesus Christ.
> ~1 Corinthians 15:55–57~

A soloist in our church sang the following song a few weeks after Mom's diagnosis. In God's providence, she was supposed to sing this on November 1, 2015, the Sunday Mom collapsed, completely unresponsive (the first clue we had that Mom was not healthy). Instead of singing that night in church, this faithful lady sat beside us in the emergency room. These words were such a challenge to me when she sang them weeks later. I love how the authors understood the reality of darkest nights in the valley coupled with the joy of experiencing only the shadow of death.

> Tender Shepherd, Sovereign Lord,
> Lead me now when life is hard,
> In Your goodness fully rest,
> Freely trust Your purposes.
> Lift my gaze from dark despair,
> Sin and sorrow reigning here,
> To the Gospel's glorious light,
> Empty tomb, victorious Christ!
>
> Refrain:
> This is my prayer, my prayer.
> In my trial, this my prayer.
>
> Loving Father, Faithful One,
> Give the weary strength to run!
> Let me see the Lamb anew
> Keeping silence when accused,
> Casting every right aside,
> Laying down His very life.
> Like my Savior, let me trust
> God the Judge, forever just.

Valley of the Shadow

God-Who-Sees, Emmanuel,
Bring me through affliction well.
Let my broken heart embrace
What You're teaching me through pain.
Move me closer to the cross,
Through the grief and through the loss,
Till from sorrow I can say,
"Christ exalted, Jesus praised!"

"A Prayer in Trial"
Words by Hannah Schopf & Heather Schopf,
© Copyright 2015 Forever Be Sure Publishing (2018 assigned to Fred Bock Music Company)
All rights reserved. Used by permission.

CHAPTER 2
PRAISE AND THANKSGIVING

An Encourager and Example

The first two chapters of this book cover the two foundational lessons God taught me in the valley of the shadow. These two lessons set the groundwork for all the other lessons God was going to teach me. The lesson in Chapter 1 was learned in stages throughout the journey and grasped more fully through studying Scripture. The lesson in this chapter was introduced to me by my cousin and then lived out by my dad. God used my cousin and Dad to teach me the stabilizing power of praise and thanksgiving in the night watches of life.

A short time before my valley journey began, my cousin gave me a challenge her mentor had given her. The challenge was simple: Long before an answer or outcome to a problem or situation is speculated or known, thank God for the fact He will answer, provide, protect, and guide. According to my cousin, this spirit of thanksgiving would completely transform my attitude and prayer life. She was right.

I then watched Dad take this truth and drive it home in real time through every one of his prayers during his valley journey. Scriptures I had known since childhood came alive as I watched Dad respond to this season of life that, humanly speaking, had come too soon for him and Mom. As I took time to ponder the myriad of verses on thanksgiving and praise and to watch Dad's response, God started a revival in my own heart. Then one day the humanly impossible happened. I was able to say, "Thank You, Lord, for cancer."

Psalm 34

Christmas Eve 2015 my family gathered around a hospital bed. Tears flowed as the word *tumor* became our new reality. Before we all went our separate ways for the night, my brother read Psalm 34. This psalm is now a best friend of mine. The first three verses speak of praise and thanksgiving.

> 1 I will bless the Lord at all times; His praise shall continually be in my mouth.
> 2 My soul makes its boast in the Lord; let the humble hear and be glad.
> 3 Oh, magnify the Lord with me, and let us exalt His name together!

There is an interesting progression in these verses. In verse 1, David's praise was a personal act before God. In verse 2, he had an audience. *Strong's Concordance* translates the word *humble* as *afflicted*.[1] These afflicted ones heard David's praise and became glad. In verse 3, David invited the afflicted ones to join him in his praise service.

Mom extended her invitation to me shortly after her diagnosis. She encouraged me to fold a piece of paper in half, write the word *cancer* on the top of one half and the word *blessings* on the top of the other. She then told me that the only negative part of her diagnosis was cancer. All the other things to follow would be praiseworthy blessings from God. I eventually realized that cancer needed to switch sides and go under the blessings side of the list, because without cancer none of the other blessings would have followed.

Fear vs. Praise

As I started to look for reasons to praise in my valley of the shadow, I discovered that often my fears would drown out my praise. Mom's diagnosis forced both of us to face our greatest fears. Mom's greatest fear had always been a brain tumor. My greatest fear had been losing a parent. These fears could have paralyzed us. How was I supposed to turn my fears into praise?

We are all familiar with the paralyzing fears of children. As a youngster, a child might need his dad to look under his bed every night to make sure no monsters are there. As he grows, this child no longer fears the unknowns under the bed. The child will eventually mature to the point where even the real yet unknown dangers of life are less fearful to him than the joys of experiencing something new—for example, driving a car for the first time.

Like that child, I was fearful because my faith was (and still is) growing. As I continually read my Bible during my valley journey, my faith was strengthened, and my fears turned into praise and thanksgiving. My praise, thanksgiving, and joy in discovering more about my God drowned out my fears of the unknowns yet to come.

James spoke of the spiritual maturity that only comes from testing. The word *perfect* in James 1 means of *full age* (mature).[2]

> Count it all joy, my brothers, when you meet trials
> of various kinds, for you know that the testing of your
> faith produces steadfastness. And let steadfastness
> have its full effect, that you may be perfect and
> complete lacking in nothing.
> ~James 1:2–4~

Psalm 34 and James 1 taught me that I needed this season of fearful trial so my faith would mature.

Turning Fear to Praise

David explained his journey from fear to praise in Psalm 34:4–7.

> 4 I sought the Lord, and He answered me and delivered me from all my fears.
> 5 Those who look to Him are radiant, and their faces shall never be ashamed.
> 6 This poor man cried, and the Lord heard him and saved him out of all his troubles.
> 7 The angel of the Lord encamps around those who fear Him, and delivers them.

David faced numerous fearful situations throughout his lifetime. In verse 4, the fears of a trial overwhelmed David. He brought his troubles to God, and God preserved him. The words *delivered* in verse 4 and *saved* in verse 6 indicate God's preservation.[3] In verse 5, David turned his eyes away from his dreadful circumstances to gaze solely on his unchangeable God, and his countenance became radiant. In verse 6, David faced more trials, but he had learned where to go in his distress. Then a marvelous moment of growth happened in verse 7. David feared God more than the trial. David's reasoning was logical. If God was able to preserve him through the terrors of the trial, then the trial no longer held the power of fear. Only the One preserving him in the trial was fear-worthy. David responded with wholehearted praise and thanksgiving.

> Oh, taste and see that the LORD is good! Blessed
> is the man who takes refuge in Him! Oh, fear the
> LORD, you His saints, for those who fear Him have
> have no lack. The young lions suffer want and hunger;
> but those who seek the LORD lack no good thing.
> ~Psalm 34:8–9~

Mom understood this progression from fear to praise. After her diagnosis, I asked her if she was still afraid of dying from a brain tumor. Mom laughed through her tears and shook her head. She had learned what I was about to learn.

In the midst of the battlefield of death, God promised to encamp around me (Psalm 34:7). He was in complete control of what had been my greatest fear—the death of a parent. He would not let death conquer Mom. In fact, not only was He in control, He was keeping the full experience of death at bay allowing Mom to only experience a shadow of it (Chapter 1). When I realized that the greatest thing I feared was completely controlled by God, I was no longer paralyzed by dread. Instead I wanted to fear the One who was powerful enough to make death obey His command and be the vehicle by which Mom would see God face-to-face (Chapters 1 and 4). Jesus shared this truth with His disciples right before He sent them out to witness to their own people.

> And do not fear those who kill the body
> but cannot kill the soul. Rather fear Him
> who can destroy both soul and body in hell.
> ~Matthew 10:28~

My fears dissipated, and I had much to give thanks for. God controlled all circumstances—even death. Therefore, nothing was fear-worthy except Him (Psalm 34:7). By focusing on God's character and His present and future answers to prayers, my praise could be louder than my fears. The fear of the Lord gave me the freedom to give thanks amid the tears of good-bye.

Focus on God's Character

David filled Psalm 34 with attributes of God that helped me look to and fear the Lord (Psalm 34:5, 7). These traits gave me stability in the midst of my fearful valley journey. Here are some of the character traits I found.

- God's goodness: "Oh, taste and see that the LORD is good!" (v. 8).
- God's protection: "Blessed is the man who takes refuge in Him!" (v. 8).
- God's provision: "The young lions suffer want and hunger; but those who seek the LORD lack no good thing" (v. 10).
- God's sovereignty: "The eyes of the LORD are toward the righteous" (v. 15).
- God's attentiveness: "And His ears toward their cry" (v. 15).
- God's justice: "The face of the LORD is against those who do evil, to cut off the memory of them from the earth" (v. 16).
- God's presence: "The LORD is near to the brokenhearted" (v. 18).
- God's help: "and saves the crushed in spirit" (v. 18).[4]
- God's preservation: "Many are the afflictions of the righteous, but the LORD delivers him out of them all" (v. 19).
- God's redemption: "The LORD redeems the life of His servants; none of those who take refuge in Him will be condemned" (v. 22).

As I meditated on His character, God quieted my fearful heart. Soon the overwhelming fears of the valley of the shadow of death were replaced with praise as I thanked God for Who He was and what He was doing in and through my family.

Focus on God's Blessings and Answers

There was great value in rehearsing God's many blessings and answers to prayer during the fearful valley journey. Mom understood this, and she asked that a record be kept of all that God was doing for our family during the last thirteen months of her life. As I started my own record of these things, I found that my fears were silenced as my focus was directed away from the fears of the future to the God who was faithfully and specifically working in all the circumstances of my life. A few of these blessings and answers to prayer are listed below.

Blessings

- Dad and Mom moved to Indianapolis a year and a half before Mom's diagnosis. Their new home was minutes away from the cancer treatment center, hospital, and several family members. Mom was able to spend the last few years of her life near family and excellent healthcare facilities.

- God provided a job for me in Indianapolis, so I was near Mom during her last few months with us.
- A family in our church, who had walked through the valley before us, provided a weekly meal for my parents.
- Another family in the church made us a huge Thanksgiving dinner when all our family was in town (and it was not Thanksgiving).
- Our family experienced the joy of belonging to the body of Christ as church families around the world told us they were praying for us.
- Coworkers prayed, cried, and rejoiced with us.
- When Mom's vision was one of the first things affected by the tumor, God provided a big-screen television through our church family. Dad and Mom were able to continue watching church services from home.
- Friends and family members sent encouraging, Scripture-filled text messages throughout the valley journey.
- Friends, who had walked this path before and understood the fears, doubts, and emotional strains of the valley journey, constantly checked in on our family.
- Books were purchased and given to us: *Don't Waste Your Cancer* by John Piper and *Off Script: What To Do When God Rewrites Your Life* by Gary Schmidt.
- A friend provided a paid-in-full photo shoot for our family.
- Mom had complete peace when confronted with her greatest fear.
- The wonderful gift of laughter saw us through many hospital visits, our last Christmas together, and the ever-so-special everyday visits in between.
- We had the opportunity to say good-bye.

Answers to Prayer

- Mom's chemotherapy pills ($1,000 per pill) were provided at no cost to Dad and Mom.
- Medi-Share® paid a huge amount of the medical costs. The numbers were large enough to make us gasp.
- A season of stunted growth in the tumor allowed Mom to meet her future son-in-law and her new grandson, to be part of a few more family events, and to enjoy some fun dates with Dad.
- Medications successfully dealt with many symptoms and allowed Mom and our family to enjoy a few more family gatherings before her passing.

- Knowledgeable and gifted medical personnel put us at ease.
- Mom maintained a sweet testimony of humor and grace during her hospital and chemo visits.
- Dad was completely free from sickness throughout the course of Mom's journey.
- At one point during our valley journey, I prayed that God would wake others up at night to pray for our family so we could get some much-needed sleep. He did just that. (May you all be granted many years of deep sleep now!)
- God gave safety. Our family traveled many miles during this time. One particular answer to prayer was Mom's safe transport to the hospital via an ambulance during an ice storm.
- On January 22, 2017, God answered Mom's childhood request for salvation. "The LORD redeemed the life of His servant, [Deborah Lewis]; she took her refuge in Him and was not condemned" (Psalm 34:22).

Thank God for Future Answers

Once I spent time focusing on God's character and the many blessings and answers to prayer He sent my way to temper the heartaches of the valley, it was time to stretch my faith by thanking God for future answers—the challenge my cousin had given me before my journey began.

Throughout my valley journey, I found myself requesting answers for current needs without praising God for the future answers He would give. *How could I praise God for an answer I wasn't sure I would like or think was good? How could I thank God now if He was going to answer with a "no"?* The words of the father in Mark 9 came to mind often. This man asked the disciples to deliver his son from an evil spirit. When the disciples could not meet this need, he turned to Jesus with the problem. The evil spirit then sent his son into convulsions right there in front of the crowd. Jesus challenged the man's faith with the words, "…All things are possible for one who believes" (v. 23).

I can hear the desperation in the father's heart as he responded: "Immediately the father of the child cried out and said, 'I believe; help my unbelief!'" (v. 24). How much like this father I was and still am.

I turned (and still turn) quickly to humans for answers. When they failed to meet the need of the moment, I turned to God. I rehearsed what God had done in the past and pondered His amazing character, but I still experienced doubts. So all I could say was "Lord, I believe. Help my unbelief. Help me to accept Your future answer as good and perfect for me. Thank You that You are unhindered by time and space, so this request is as good as answered. Thank You that You will answer this in the best way for both my good and Your glory!" I then found that my fears of the future grew smaller as my eager anticipation of what God was going to do grew greater.

The transformation from fear to praise and thanksgiving was not easy. I have and will continue to experience many failed attempts along the way. Oh, that I would always pursue a lifestyle of praise and thanksgiving so I can reflect the joyful heart of the Proverbs 31 woman.

> She is clothed with strength and dignity,
> and she laughs without fear of the future.
> ~Proverbs 31:25~

Johnson Oatman summarized the value of rehearsing God's blessings and answers to prayer in his hymn "Count Your Blessings." These words often come to mind as I learned to give thanks in my valley journey.

> When upon life's billows you are tempest tossed,
> When you are discouraged, thinking all is lost,
> Count your many blessings, name them one by one,
> And it will surprise you what the Lord hath done.

> Refrain:
> Count your blessings, name them one by one,
> Count your blessings, see what God has done!
> Count your blessings, name them one by one,
> Count your many blessings, see what God has done.

> Are you ever burdened with a load of care?
> Does the cross seem heavy you are called to bear?
> Count your many blessings, every doubt will fly,
> And you will keep singing as the days go by.

> So amid the conflict whether great or small,
> Do not be discouraged, God is overall;
> Count your many blessings, angels will attend,
> Help and comfort give you to your journey's end.

"Count Your Blessings"
Words by Johnson Oatman, Jr., 1856–1922

CHAPTER 3
VALLEY OF TEARS

Psalm 23 taught me that my valley journey was but a shadow of death. Psalm 34 taught me how to quiet my fears by giving thanks at all times. These truths caused me to wonder if the heart-wrenching sorrow of the valley of the shadow should still exist for the believer. Were gut-wrenching heartaches and tears acceptable in the valley? God used Psalm 84 and 1 Thessalonians 4 to teach me that He gives the believer freedom to grieve.

Psalm 84

Psalm 84 is a favorite of mine because it recognizes the reality and benefit of both tears and joy in the believer's life. The recognition of this reality gave me great freedom to grieve, even in the midst of one of the happiest moments of my life.

    My brother read Psalm 84 at my wedding. Those in attendance were keenly aware of the two empty seats beside Dad and my soon-to-be Dad-in-law. Both men had lost their wives in the last year and a half to the same type of brain cancer. Two red roses sat on either side of our unity candle representing our dear sweet Moms, who never truly understood our love for each other because brain cancer took away their memory and comprehension. My husband's two sisters-in-law were present. These dear ladies stood next to Todd when he married their older sister in 2002 and then again when he buried her in 2013. While there was great joy at the joining together of our two lives, there were tears also—tears over the vacancies left by those who were now in heaven. It was a bittersweet day for many—a day full of life's realities of sorrow and joy.

In the valley journey, life is emotional. Period. There is no way around it. Many of the months I spent in the valley, I was saying good-bye to my mother while getting to know the man I would marry. Tears were never far away even on the happiest occasions. Many times, smiles were accompanied by tears. Psalm 84 taught me that God welcomes tears.

> As they go through the Valley of Baca they make
> it a place of springs; the early rain also covers it
> with pools. They go from strength to strength;
> each one appears before God in Zion.
> ~Psalm 84:6–7~

Baca is the Hebrew word for *weeping*.[5] The psalmist recognized the realities of life's heartaches by using the phrase "the valley of weeping" in verse 6.

Tears of Reality

My tears were a reminder of the harsh reality of disease. I cried as I watched cancer take away Mom's ability to play the piano, read a book, and take a walk with Dad.

My tears were a reminder of an upcoming painful good-bye. There was a day coming when Mom would no longer be a part of our family gatherings. She would be sorely missed. Dad reminded me that a heart-wrenching farewell meant Mom had a made a difference in my life.

My tears were in recognition of dreams never fulfilled. Mom would not be present for my engagement, wedding, or the announcement of Baby Townsend.

My tears were a reminder that life was forever changing and would never be the same again. I would never again hear her voice on the other end of the telephone or hear her play the piano or hear her say she was praying for me.

Sometimes I would tear up for a second or two before pulling myself together. Sometimes the tears came with gut-wrenching sobs that silently shook my body as I curled up in a ball in the privacy of my own home. Sometimes the tears were accompanied with soft sobs as I took a much needed walk outside. Sometimes the tears would flow at my desk at work when no one was around after I read an encouraging text from a friend. There were and still are many tears. Does any good come from this intense emotion? *Yes*! The psalmist speaks of this good in Psalm 84.

Tears of Sorrow and Strength

The valley of tears is a place of sorrow, but it is also a place of springs (Psalm 84:6). Springs offer nourishment and refreshment—each needed to strengthen me in future days.

I love verse 7: "They go from strength to strength." The tears of sorrow from yesterday's trials become the source of strength for today's trials. What a comforting thought! The weeping of my valley journey was not in vain. Yet how could I ensure my tears of sorrow would be tears of strength stored up to help me through future trials? The wise man's response in Ecclesiastes 7 gave me the answer.

> It is better to go to the house of mourning than
> to go to the house of feasting, for this is the end
> of all mankind, and the living will lay it to heart.
> ~Ecclesiastes 7:2~

When I allowed my tears of sorrow to instruct rather than overwhelm me, I discovered tears of strength. I needed (and still need) to take to heart the lessons found in the grief experienced at a funeral. Tears of sorrow taught me to number my days (Psalm 90:12) so I would live wisely. Tears of sorrow taught me to make adjustments to my living. I needed to prioritize and organize my life so that I was preparing for my permanent home—heaven (Hebrews 11:13–16; Matthew 6:19–21). I learned that my life is but a short breath (James 4:13–15), so I must invest it well.

When I allowed my tears to instruct me in wise living, I drew strength for the coming days. In the future, I will draw from the deep waters of sorrow experienced in the valley of the shadow of death to encourage others and help me through different trials.

1 Thessalonians 4

Sometimes 1 Thessalonians 4:13 is quoted to those who are grieving, and instead of the clear comfort this verse should give, the one grieving can sink into a sticky mire of guilt and fear if this verse is not understood in its context. When this verse was quoted to me, I was often fearful that others thought I was grieving as "others who have no hope." I did not want to dishonor God by my tears (see Chapter 6).

> But we do not want you to be uninformed,
> brothers, about those who are asleep, that you
> may not grieve as others do who have no hope.

Tears of Fear

This verse was written to correct a faulty viewpoint that led to great confusion among the Thessalonian believers.[6] The confusion was about Jesus's imminent return. The Thessalonian believers were convinced that Jesus was coming back in their lifetime. They experienced great confusion as they watched loved ones who had trusted Christ as Savior die before Christ's return. Would these loved ones still experience Christ's second return and their promised salvation? The Thessalonians were also experiencing great persecution for their faith, and this added to their confusion and fears. Paul explained the second coming of Christ in the verses following verse 13 and helped still their fears by cementing their feet in truth.

Today I have the full revelation of scriptural truth, so the false feelings of guilt and fear that came when others quote these verses were not mine to bear. Paul corrected the thinking of the Thessalonians believers, and their fears were calmed as they understood that their loved ones' future was secure despite the chaos and turmoil around them. My fears of dishonoring God with my grief were calmed as I realized that this passage gave me freedom to weep because I had known the truths of 1 Thessalonians 4 since I was a child.

Tears of Hope and Absence

Once I understood the context of 1 Thessalonians 4:13, I no longer experienced guilt or fear when this verse was shared with me. I have never once, since her death, doubted where Mom is. The grief I experienced in the valley of the shadow was because of the absence of Mom here on earth, not because I feared for her spiritual well-being. The grief of absence was not the same as "grieving as those who have no hope."

Mom expressed this same grief—the grief of absence. She hurt for us and the pain we were about to experience when she left. She grieved over the engagements, weddings, family gatherings, births, and other events she would miss. Yet Mom's steadfast hope in God's ability to keep His promise to save her soul never wavered.

Mom could not wait to reach heaven. As I shared with you in Chapter 1, during Mom's last Christmas, she eagerly asked me, "Jenn, have you heard where I am going?" At that moment I cried tears of hope and absence. Tears of hope because Mom would soon be face-to-face with Jesus—oh, what that must be like! Tears of absence because soon she would leave an empty place here on earth that no one else could fill. Because of the truth revealed in the context of 1 Thessalonians 4, I had freedom to weep.

Psalm 139

Psalm 139 captures the beauty of God's personal involvement in forming each human being. He created each individual uniquely different from all others. These differences need to be understood and appreciated during difficult times.

> For You formed my inward parts; You knitted me together in my mother's womb. I praise You, for I am fearfully and wonderfully made. Wonderful are Your works; my soul knows it very well. My frame was not hidden from You, when I was being made in secret, intricately woven in the depths of the earth. Your eyes saw my unformed substance; in Your book were written, every one of them, the days that were formed for me, when as yet there was none of them.
> ~Psalm 139:13–16~

Tears of Personality

Eighteen people in our immediate family walked through the valley of the shadow of death. After observing each of us walk this path, I am convinced that there must be at least eighteen different ways to grieve. As our family cried together, I learned that grief is a personal journey. Each family member responded differently to the many valley challenges we faced. Our tears were a gift from God given at the time that was right for each of us. The tenderness of one's heart and the emotional maturity of one's mind could not be determined by the abundance or lack of tears at a given moment. As a family, we appreciated and loved each one's unique God-given personality, and we learned to give each other space to grieve accordingly.

God's Promises for the Brokenhearted

Dear reader, we can cry those tender tears of reality, sorrow and strength, hope and absence, and personality. Our tears are a reminder of the reality of an ever-changing life. Our tears of sorrow will become tears of strength that will provide nourishment and refreshment for both us and others in coming days. Our tears of hope in the reality of heaven will balance our tears of absence. God sees our tears and hears our cries. He promises that our tears are not forgotten. I hope these promises are an encouragement to your grieving heart today.

For everything there is a season…a time to weep, and
a time to laugh; a time to mourn, and a time to dance;…
~Ecclesiastes 3:1, 4~

You have kept count of my tossings; put my
tears in your bottle. Are they not in your book?
~Psalm 56:8~

The eyes of the Lord are toward the
righteous and His ears toward their cry.
~Psalm 34:15~

The Lord is near to the brokenhearted
and saves the crushed in spirit.
~Psalm 34:18~

In my distress I called upon the Lord; to my
God I cried for help. From His temple He heard
my voice, and my cry to Him reached His ears.
~Psalm 18:6~

CHAPTER 4
THE LIVING WORD OF GOD

The emotions of the valley of the shadow—tears of reality, sorrow and strength, hope and absence, and personality—were draining. But God's Word proved to be more than enough to give hope to my hurting heart, peace to my distressed mind, and comfort to my overwhelmed soul.

The Sufficiency of Scripture

I memorized Bible verses as a child. I sang hymns as a teenager. I heard my parents' constant reminders. I took notes during Pastor's many sermons. I had, at various moments in college, experienced in a small way the truth of the powerful, living nature of God's Word. I had quoted the words "His Word is a lamp unto my feet" (Psalm 119:105) many times, but until November 2015 I had yet to grasp the all-sufficient nature of the Bible and my overwhelming need for it.

> For the word of God is living and active, sharper than any two-edged sword, piercing to the division of soul and of spirit, of joints and of marrow, and discerning the thoughts and intentions of the heart.
> ~Hebrews 4:12~

> All Scripture is breathed out by God and profitable for teaching, for reproof, for correction, and for training in righteousness, that the man of God may be complete, equipped for every good work.
> ~2 Timothy 3:16–17~

Throughout my valley journey, God brought me to situations in which no earthly form of help was available. In those moments I was forced to turn to Scripture. The only answers were found in His promises, His names, and different statements from Scripture. God used these to provide the comfort, wisdom, explanation, or principle I needed. As I read Scripture and watched God work through His Word, my need for the Bible became more and more apparent. Now, months later, I understand personally the great need that led Job to say:

> I have not departed from the commandment
> of His lips; I have treasured the words of
> His mouth more than my portion of food.
> ~Job 23:12~

God's Promised Presence

Background

November 1, 2015, was the date that forever changed my understanding of God's presence. Mom had collapsed, unresponsive, that afternoon and had been rushed to the emergency room. Dad sat by Mom's side as seizures rocked her body. My sister and I sat anxiously in the waiting room. Needing a moment away from people, I found refuge in a bathroom stall and started to sob. My words at that time were so simple, yet they changed my focus from that moment forward: "God, Mom belongs to You. Do whatever You wish with her; but please, please never leave me nor forsake me. If You leave me, I cannot go on." The peace that pervaded an obscure bathroom stall in Community Hospital North was tangible.

The Living Word of God

My prayer that day came directly from a verse I had learned as a child.

> Keep your life free from love of money, and
> be content with what you have, for He has said,
> "I will never leave you nor forsake you." So we
> can confidently say, "The Lord is my helper; I
> will not fear; what can man do to me?"
> ~Hebrews 13:5–6~

In the weeks and months to follow, I would struggle as I came to grips with many spiritual truths I had taken for granted in the previous thirty-six years of my life, but I would never doubt God's presence. God was as close as a whispered, "Help." In my moments of greatest distress, He reminded me again that He would never leave or forsake me. Mom left me because her task on earth was done, but God did not leave me. Someday each of my family members will leave me. I will one day leave my husband and children; but God will never leave any of His children.

This simple truth of God's continual presence gave me wisdom in the toughest decisions, peace in the horrific moments of cancer, comfort when human comfort was not enough, and hope when life appeared hopeless. The statement, "I will never leave you," held many personal moments of testimony—moments where God made Himself real to me and showed me that He was intensely involved in every detail of my life. He was never too busy or too preoccupied to leave His daughter alone in her journey. He kept His promise.

God's Promised Help

Background

It was a Friday evening. The work week had been long and difficult, and I was completely overwhelmed. I made the decision to head over to my parents' house. Surely there I would find some sense of calm and be able to refocus.

I walked into the house, and it became apparent that it had been a long, hard day for Mom. Within a few minutes, I realized that my presence was causing more angst for Mom than help. The cancer had progressed far enough into her brain to affect her sense of peace and her personality. I did what I could to help and then told Dad I would head home and let Mom have some of her "normal" setting back. I hoped this would give her some peace, and Dad agreed that was probably the best decision.

My drive back home was quiet and lonely. As I got to my apartment, I decided to call Todd. We were dating at the time and knew that marriage was on the horizon. Surely I would find some relief from the frustrations and discouragement of the week by talking to this man that I had come to love.

As soon as Todd picked up the phone, I could hear the discouragement in his voice. He was going through Naomi's (his first wife's) belongings. The memories were overwhelming, and he needed a friend. He put down the phone to go get something, and I had a moment to myself. I put my phone down and the overwhelming nature of the week rushed on me like a tsunami wave. I began sobbing. "Lord, I can't do this anymore. Every area of my life is beyond me this year. I have no clue how to handle the frustrations at work, the ever-changing nature of Mom's cancer, or the grief of watching this man I love relive the loss of his first wife as he goes through her belongings. Help!" Immediately the peace of God surrounded me, and the tears stopped.

The Living Word of God

In that moment two verses flooded my overwhelmed mind.

> Casting all your anxieties on Him,
> because He cares for you.
> ~1 Peter 5:7~

> Come to me, all who labor and are heavy
> laden, and I will give you rest. Take my yoke
> upon you, and learn from Me, for I am gentle
> and lowly in heart, and you will find rest for your
> souls. For My yoke is easy, and My burden is light.
> ~Matthew 11:28–30~

The Jewish religion of Jesus's day was based on strict adherence to many man-made laws and rules.[7] This legalistic system taught that good works would earn God's approval. Jesus offered a religion that was based on a relationship, not works, because He finished the work for me on the cross (Matthew 11:28–30). The continuation of that relationship was not based on works but on a growing friendship—a friendship in which I allowed God to place on my shoulders the yoke for each day that He deemed best. I realized He would walk alongside me and help me bear that load—the load chosen by God to be exactly what I needed for the day.

But what was I supposed to do when the load was too heavy for me because I was carrying too much? The passage in Peter encouraged me to cast my overwhelming cares on God that night. He had saved me; He would carry these burdens too. God would carry the burdens of work and Mom's cancer that night if I just handed them to Him. In that moment of time, I was with Todd, and my focus needed to be on him. My prayer of praise expressed the relief that these verses brought me that evening: "God, thank You! I finally understand what these verses mean. You will carry Mom and work. I'll let You carry those burdens tonight. I am going to focus on Todd."

In the one minute Todd was gone from the phone, I had come to a practical understanding of two precious passages of Scripture. I could rest in God's care and meet the needs that were in front of me while He helped me carry the other burdens He had placed on me for that day. Todd and I talked most of that evening. He went through many of his first wife's belongings while we laughed much, cried some, and had a wonderful time together.

God's promises were stabilizing truths in the midst of the roller-coaster emotions of the valley. I also found great comfort in the names of God. His various names helped me understand who He is and how He relates to His people in dark times. Two of these names brought me much comfort the day of Mom's diagnosis.

God's Names

Background

Christmas Eve is my favorite day of the year. In years past Christmas Eve had held a sort of magic for me. The story of the shepherds being the first Bethlehem residents to hear the news of Emmanuel's arrival had fascinated me. I had always loved the Christmas Eve candlelight services. It was as though the whole world was waiting for the angels to start singing again. Hearing the last chords of "Silent Night" in church just before walking outside to snow softly falling around me made the day picture perfect. It was always the one day of the year that nothing could spoil.

On Christmas Eve night of 2015, we gathered around Mom's hospital bed. Dad told us that Mom had a brain tumor. We cried, hugged, and cried some more. We read Psalm 34 together. In the midst of this emotional evening, God would bring peace to my heart and mind through two names for Jesus.

The Living Word of God

When I arrived home that night, I was unable to sleep. I knew that the news of a brain tumor could forever ruin Christmas Eve for me, so I asked God to teach me to still love this day. Yes, the magic was forever gone; but there had to be something else about Christmas Eve that captivated me so I would not lose the joy of this day in future years. As the night hours ticked away, I thought about two names for Jesus that are often mentioned during the Christmas season —Emmanuel (the Hebrew word is *Immanuel*) and Prince of Peace.

> "Behold, the virgin shall conceive and bear a
> son, and they shall call his name Immanuel"
> (which means, God with us).
> ~Matthew 1:23~

> For to us a Child is born, to us a Son is given;
> and the government shall be upon His shoulder,
> and His name shall be called Wonderful Counselor,
> Mighty God, Everlasting Father, Prince of Peace.
> ~Isaiah 9:6~

Emmanuel means "God with us." The very reason Emmanuel came to live with us on earth at Christmas is explained by Jesus's name Prince of Peace. God dwelled with us so He could bring us eternal peace. The magic of Christmas Eve that held me spellbound as a child was replaced by the security that God had planned so great a salvation for me. Not only did God (Emmanuel) visit the shepherds in the beauty of Christmas, but He (the Prince of Peace) endured the horrors of the cross and caused me to triumph over sin and death at the empty tomb on Easter weekend.

Now Christmas Eve holds such a sweet and vivid reminder of my salvation. This was the day Mom began the last chapter of her salvation story—her walk to eternal life promised by her Savior at the moment of her salvation. All because the Emmanuel of Christmas Eve was the Prince of Peace of Easter, Mom rests in His presence today. Oh, the joy and security of Christmas Eve!

As I claimed God's promises and studied His names, I began to gain a deeper understanding and appreciation of other statements and stories from Scripture. One of those passages provided overwhelming comfort in one of the most terrifying paths I encountered in my valley of the shadow journey. Several other passages provided stabilizing truths many months later, when one of the most agonizing aspects of death visited our family.

God's Salvation

Of all the sections in this book, this was one of the hardest to write. It was the most humbling path of the journey and one of the darkest times in my valley. After months of an agonizing struggle with the most basic tenets of my faith, the truth of God's Word provided concrete answers for the overwhelming doubts that were plaguing my soul.

Background

Our church leadership had asked two of my siblings and me to provide a video testimonial which would be shared during the morning Easter service on March 27, 2016. We were asked to share how the truth of the resurrection sustained us during difficult days. We each choose a different section or verse from Psalm 34 to share. My testimony was as follows:

How does the resurrection of Jesus bring confidence?

"My soul makes its boast in the LORD;
let the humble hear and be glad."
~Psalm 34:2~

The word *humble* means *afflicted*.[8] My Savior experienced the worst kind of affliction possible—separation from God the Father. Why did He do this? Scripture says it was "for the joy that was set before Him" (Hebrews 12:2). His joy was in securing my future state—eternity in heaven. The worst affliction I would ever have to face was absorbed in Christ so the momentary afflictions of this life are light and tempered for me as His child.

The word *LORD* is in all caps throughout Psalm 34. This name references God's self-existent and eternal nature.[9] The Self-Existent One has conquered death and is the personification of Eternity (time without beginning or end). The Self-Existent One, who suffered the greatest affliction possible, pierced hell's darkness and death's horrors with His triumphant mercy, grace, and love. He can and He will (for He has promised) pierce my darkest of earthly nights with that same mercy, grace, and love.

There is no danger, darkness, or fear that I, as His child, must face alone. He reaches His hand out over our darkest moments of life and says, "Dear one, I was afflicted for your sake. For your sake I was separated from My heavenly Father, and for your sake I conquered that which the medical field cannot stop and what academia cannot reason with. *I have conquered death.* I will walk with you through this affliction as well."

And so, with our adoring eyes fixed on our Savior in the midst of this affliction, our family cries out with the security of greatest confidence, "My soul will make its boast in the LORD, the humble shall hear and be glad" (Psalm 34:2). Be glad with me today. Because He lives, He is our confidence in difficult times.

When I wrote these words for our testimonial, I had no doubt of the security of my eternal state or the reality of eternity in heaven for those who believe in the life, death, burial, and resurrection of Jesus. However, in the weeks between the filming of this testimony and Easter Sunday when it was played, my heart had become overwhelmed with doubts. I entered church that Easter morning with dread.

I was strangled by doubts: *What if Jesus is a myth? What if what I've believed and followed my whole life is actually a cult? What if Mom doesn't go to heaven when she dies? What if all the things I've believed since I was thirteen are just sweet beliefs, but there is no life after death?*

I had been an educator in Christian schools for thirteen years. I had been teaching adult women during Sunday School for several years. I had been going to church since I was a baby. My closest friends were all believers. To doubt the basic tenets of my faith shook me to my core. The doubts continued for weeks. God used Pastor's Easter sermon that year to speak directly to my hurting and fearful heart.

The Living Word of God

Pastor preached from 1 Corinthians 15 that morning.

> I tell you this, brothers: flesh and blood cannot inherit the kingdom of God, nor does the perishable inherit the imperishable. Behold! I tell you a mystery. We shall not all sleep, but we shall all be changed, in a moment, in the twinkling of an eye, at the last trumpet. For the trumpet will sound, and the dead will be raised imperishable, and we shall be changed. For this perishable body must put on the imperishable, and this mortal body must put on immortality. When the perishable puts on the the imperishable, and the mortal puts on immortality, then shall come to pass the saying that is written:
>
> "Death is swallowed up in victory."
> "O death, where is your victory?
> O death, where is your sting?"
>
> The sting of death is sin, and the power of sin is the law. But thanks be to God, who gives us the victory through our Lord Jesus Christ. Therefore, my beloved, brothers be steadfast, immovable, always abounding in the work of the Lord, knowing that in the Lord your labor is not in vain.
> ~1 Corinthians 15:50–58~

The phrase "this perishable body must put on the imperishable" struck me and brought immediate peace. It would take many months of studying these verses to understand why that immediate peace came, but the doubts were gone. I had no reason to doubt the validity of what I had been taught. As I studied this passage, I began to understand that the very thing that was causing my doubt (the process of death) was God's way of building my confidence in Him. He was keeping His promise to Mom.

Through the process of death, God was visibly removing the perishable from Mom—that which was limited by sin and affected by disease (a result of sin). He was then going to replace it with the imperishable—that which was created for heaven. Physical death was the last step of ensuring that Mom would be home in heaven with God forever. God was, in my very presence, showing me how He changed the perishable to imperishable to ensure Mom's full salvation.

I could now be "steadfast and immovable" in my faith (v. 58) amid the changes Mom experienced in the process of death. This process was not meant to bring doubts or fears but to bring assurance that God sees the labor of His child and keeps His Word. When the labor of His child is done, He will, without fail, do His part to replace mortality with immortality.

Once again, God's Word powerfully worked in my life during a season of great struggle and gave me the peace needed to face the coming months with no doubts sabotaging my faith. Months later, as the brain cancer progressed, God used another passage of Scripture to bring great peace to my heart as I watched this disease continue to rid Mom of her perishable body.

God's Love

Background

There was a time during Mom's battle with cancer when the tumor had progressed far enough into her brain to affect her personality and peace of mind (see Chapter 5). Although she had spent her life saturating her mind with Scripture and discipling her mind to think biblically, Mom had no power over the cancer and what it did to her mind. Those who have watched Alzheimer's disease progress in their loved ones understand the agony of this progression.

Scripture verses I had learned as a child, reassured me that God was merciful, understood the frailty of the human mind, and would keep His promises.

The Living Word of God

God was and is greater than any disease that ever attacked the feeble, finite minds of His children. No end-of-life disease would cause my God to revoke His promises to His children. Death, in all its horror, could never stay God's hand. Paul spoke of this incredibly stabilizing truth in Romans.

> For I am sure that neither death nor life, nor angels
> nor rulers, nor things present nor things to come,
> nor powers, nor height nor depth, nor anything else
> in all creation, will be able to separate us from the
> love of God in Christ Jesus our Lord.
> ~Romans 8:38–39~

In Psalm 103, David also spoke of God's preserving love and care for His children despite their sinful natures.

> For as high as the heavens are above the earth,
> so great is His steadfast love toward those who
> fear Him; as far as the east is from the west, so
> far does He remove our transgressions from us.
> As a father shows compassion to his children, so
> the Lord shows compassion to those who fear
> Him. For He knows our frame; He remembers
> that we are dust.
> ~Psalm 103:11–14~

The writer of Hebrews spoke of Jesus's priesthood duties. His duties did not cease when cancer robbed Mom of her ability to think logically or biblically. He had "saved her to the uttermost" and lived in that moment to intercede before God on her behalf.

> But He holds His priesthood permanently,
> because He continues forever. Consequently, He
> is able to save to the uttermost those who draw
> near to God through Him, since He always lives
> to make intercession for them.
> ~Hebrews 7:24–25~

What incredibly stabilizing verses to focus on during those difficult days! When Mom's mind was no longer under her control, Mom was still God's child. God had not lost control of His plans or His child, and He faithfully kept His promises to her.

Throughout all generations, the living nature of God's Word has set this book apart from all other books. The Bible has always revealed what God has done, is doing, and will do in the world to accomplish His great purposes. The Psalmist understood the unparalleled value of God's Word when he penned the entire chapter of Psalm 119.

The Living Word of God

Open my eyes, that I may behold wondrous
things out of Your law. I am a sojourner on the
earth; hide not Your commandments from me!
~vv. 18–19~

Your testimonies are my delight; they are
my counselors. My soul clings to the dust;
give me life according to Your word!
~vv. 24–25~

Turn my eyes from looking at worthless things;
and give me life in your ways. Confirm to Your
servant Your promise, that You may be feared.
~vv. 37–38~

Let Your steadfast love come to me, O Lord,
Your salvation according to Your promise;…
~v. 41~

This is my comfort in my affliction,
that Your promise gives me life.
~v. 50~

The LORD is my portion;
I promise to keep Your words.
~v. 57~

You have dealt well with Your servant,
O LORD, according to Your word.
~v. 65~

It is good for me that I was afflicted, that I
might learn Your statutes. The law of Your
mouth is better to me than thousands of
gold and silver pieces.
~vv. 71–72~

My soul longs for Your salvation; I hope in
Your word. My eyes long for Your promise;
I ask, "When will You comfort me?"
~vv. 81–82~

Forever, O LORD, Your word is firmly fixed
in the heavens. Your faithfulness endures to
all generations; You have established the earth,
and it stands fast. By Your appointment they stand
this day, for all things are Your servants. If Your
law had not been my delight, I would have perished
in my affliction. I will never forget Your precepts,
for by them You have given me life.
~vv. 89–93~

Your testimonies are my heritage forever,
for they are the joy of my heart.
~v. 111~

My eyes long for Your salvation and for
the fulfillment of Your righteous promise.
~v. 123~

Great peace have those who love Your law;
nothing can make them stumble.
~v. 165~

CHAPTER 5
END-OF-LIFE STORIES

God's Word proved to be my constant source of help in the ever-changing valley of the shadow journey. When Mom entered hospice and the end of her life was so different than what I had always expected, God's Word was again my source of hope and strength.

Just as everyone's birth story is unique, so everyone's end-of-life story is unique. As Mom's final days on earth approached, I wondered how her story would go. I had heard end-of-life stories that encouraged me and others that challenged me, but Mom's end-of-life story changed my perspective of God's salvation. I was grateful that God's patience never waned as He used Mom's death to help me gain a deeper appreciation for and understanding of His plan of salvation.

Stories of Encouragement

I had heard them my whole life—incredibly inspiring end-of-life stories of believers. Stories of people who, in the last moments of their life, were surrounded by loved ones singing songs of the faith. There were smiles on everyone's faces despite the tears. The departing believer would say his final words filled with great anticipation of leaving this world and going to the next. Then the loved one experienced a gentle, quiet departure from life on earth to life in heaven. In these stories, there were tears of sorrow, but the joy of the departing one lifted the spirits of those around him. These stories encouraged me to fill my mind with Scripture and spiritual songs so my parting day would be full of truth and encouragement for those left behind.

Stories of Challenge

Then there were the stories of those killed instantaneously in car accidents, or those who died from a heart attack while working out in the yard, or those who passed away unexpectedly in their sleep. These stories held their own unique heartaches of loved ones not having a chance to say good-bye, the intense pain of having a loved one ripped so unexpectedly from one's life, or losing a child before he had grown up. The comfort for me in these stories was that the one who departed struggled very little as death came quickly. These stories challenged me to cherish every minute with family and not let anger or petty differences come between me and my family and friends.

Stories of Perspective

Then there were the stories I heard only from dear friends. Many of those friends could not verbalize these stories until long after their loved one had passed for the memories were so painful to recall. They were careful in their wording because they did not want to dishonor the one they loved. Yet the agonizing struggles of their loved one's last days were so filled with the incredible ache of death in a sin-cursed world, and my friends longed to share their reality with others. These stories were vastly different from the sermon illustrations I wanted to experience on my loved ones' final days or the quick departure I desired at the end of my life. These stories of perspective made me eager for heaven as my friends, and eventually I, watched the consequences of living in a sin-cursed world decay the bodies of our loved ones. These stories changed my perspective of life here on earth and life in heaven.

Mom's Story

Mom's end-of-life story was one of perspective. Mom was a faithful believer in Christ during her sixty-four years on earth. She loved Jesus. Her Bible was covered in red or black comments she wrote down as she read her Bible and listened to sermons. She and Dad memorized Scripture together on a regular basis.

Mom loved Dad. When they met Dad was unsaved. Grandma Roberts, Mom's mother, had been praying for Dad's salvation for years. Mom and Grandma took Dad to an evangelistic meeting, and shortly thereafter he accepted the truth of the gospel and became a believer. Mom faithfully followed Dad after their marriage. Dad was learning much about the Bible and had many questions for Mom as he grew in his relationship with God.

Mom and Dad were best friends, and they did everything together. They went fishing and hiking, stacked wood, painted the house, mowed the lawn, lugged and burned brush, cut Christmas trees, sang around the piano, laughed at us kids, played wiffle ball, and had water fights. Together they raised a family. As God added each of us children to the family, we were included in all activities.

Mom loved her five children. She taught each of us Scripture verses as soon as we could talk. As soon as we could read, she had us reading God's Word each day. Her constant words of advice were, "Let's see what the Bible says about that." Mom always looked forward to summer when school was over and she was surrounded by her children She taught us to work hard and to enjoy every aspect of life She would spend the hours at home finding ways to serve each of us, praying for us as she cleaned the house, and making our home into a haven of rest and peace.

Mom loved God's people. She played the piano for our church, and would practice at night playing us kids to sleep with hymns for the next service. She made sure her family was at church for every possible event. She would sing throughout the day or have uplifting, encouraging music playing in the background. She also loved to read. Her bedside stand usually held a novel and a Christian-living book. Mom lived to serve others and point them to Christ. As the years passed, she was asked to speak at ladies' events on biblical child-rearing, and many ladies went to her for advice on maintaining a God-honoring home.

Then the day came when all the kids were grown, and the house was quiet. Dad and Mom followed God's leading to Indianapolis where they were finally close to some of their grandchildren. Mom loved her grandkids. However, less than three years after the move, a glioblastoma took away Mom's simplest earthly joys.

The tumor immediately impacted Mom's vision, balance, and short-term memory. She was no longer able to read books or her Bible because the words would move on the page. She could not play the piano for the same reason. Listening to Scripture on a CD was hard because she could not remember what had just been said, and the noise would bother her.

Mom's gentle godly spirit persevered through many of the changes that cancer brought. But the day finally came when the cancer took enough of her mind to affect Mom's personality. This stage was the most difficult to experience as we watched Mom's peace of mind disappear. It was during this time that Mom entered home hospice.

God graciously allowed Mom to fall asleep one day, and she slept through the remainder of her life. We were told what to expect during the last moments of life, yet God spared us from many of these worst-case scenarios. He answered our prayers and took Mom to heaven while she was sleeping. On January 22, 2017, Mom entered God's presence with a whole body and mind. She was able to see and understand God fully with no veil of earth and sin between. The One she had faithfully served had kept His promise to His daughter.

> The Lord redeems the life of His servants; none of
> those who take refuge in Him will be condemned.
> ~Psalm 34:22~

I have found that in the American Christian culture in which I live there are more end-of-life stories of perspective than encouragement or challenge. Why is that? Why did I need to watch Mom live out her perspective-changing end-of-life story? I discovered through the painful process of death I needed to consider some difficult topics that I, up to this point in my life, had avoided.

A Biblical Perspective

I have always been a generally happy, fun-loving person. I lived a comfortable American Christian life with no persecution and no major life catastrophes. I understood the struggles of adult life. I have watched churches fail and men and women walk away from the faith. I was unexpectedly laid off from work, went through a biopsy for cancer, and had to adjust my lifestyle after receiving tough medical news in my mid-twenties. I understood the challenges of creating a new department at work. I had uprooted my life and started all over again two times before my journey through the valley of the shadow. But these were all normal American Christian life scenarios that were non-life-threatening. If asked to describe my life, I would have had to use the words *good* and *pleasant*.

Due to my personality and the pleasantness of my life, I would often push the sad topics of life and death from my mind. God used the physical suffering and death of Mom to force me to consider these topics. Those dark days in the valley drove me to search God's Word for answers for the sadness I was experiencing. Not only did He provide answers, God gave joy as I gained a deeper understanding of His complete plan of salvation. This understanding came as I acknowledged the painful realities of living in a sin-cursed world, pondered the reality of heaven, and began the process of relinquishing my grip on earthly ties so I would desire the better life in heaven that God has planned for His children.

Realities of a Sin-Cursed World

Isaiah 6 speaks of the holiness (set apart nature) of God.

> In the year that King Uzziah died I saw the Lord sitting upon a throne, high and lifted up; and the train of His robe filled the temple. Above Him stood the seraphim. Each had six wings: with two he covered his face, and with two he covered his feet, and with two he flew. And one called to another and said:
>
> "Holy, holy, holy is the Lord of hosts;
> the whole earth is full of His glory!"
>
> And the foundations of the thresholds shook at the voice of him who called, and the house was filled with smoke. And I said: "Woe is me! For I am lost; for I am a man of unclean, lips and I dwell in the midst of a people of unclean lips; for my eyes have seen the King, the Lord of hosts!" Then one of the seraphim flew to me, having in his hand a burning coal that he had taken with tongs from the altar. And he touched my mouth and said: "Behold, this has touched your lips; your guilt is taken away, and your sin atoned for."
> ~Isaiah 6:1–7~

This scene was one from another world—the perfect throne room of the God of the universe. The Lord sat high and lifted up on a throne, set apart from all other beings. His train was longer than that of any bride in the history of mankind. Those attending Him were creatures specifically created to declare God's holiness. The voices of these seraphim shook the foundation of the smoke-filled room. This throne room of God was set apart from the imperfections of Isaiah's sinful world.

Isaiah saw his ugly sins and the sins of the world in which he lived next to the beauty of God's perfection and holiness and responded accordingly: "Woe is me!" His statement was a simple acknowledgement of the consequences he knew he deserved for his sin.

When Adam and Eve chose their own way over God's, they stepped away from God's intended utopia of a personal walk with Him in the serene Garden of Eden. They stepped into a world that was and is still fighting to move as far away from God and His perfect plan for mankind as possible. As a result of man's rebellion against God, cancer, Alzheimer's, gene mutations, pain, and heartache invaded the world. These were not part of God's original plan for mankind but were the consequences of sin.

Mom did not commit a particular sin that resulted in cancer. Just as the young Christian woman killed by a drunk driver or the pastor beheaded for sharing the gospel in his village, Mom lived in a sin-cursed world and experienced the pains and sorrows that come with sin. In watching Mom suffer through cancer, the realities of Romans 5 became apparent.

> Therefore, just as sin came into the world
> through one man and death through sin, and
> so death spread to all men because all sinned…
> ~Romans 5:12~

This section of the book could be deeply discouraging to read with its somber tone and harsh realities. But this difficult topic lead me to a new understanding of my homeland—heaven. The pain and suffering caused by sin forced me to reconsider the reality of heaven. One of the horrible results of living in a sin-cursed world (disease) took Mom away from this imperfect world to the perfect world of heaven.

Reality of Heaven

Before I entered the valley of the shadow, I had experienced a comfortable and pleasant life for thirty-six years, and heaven seemed like a distant land to me. When Grandma Roberts died, it became more real, but it still did not hold the same reality earth held. As Mom neared the end of her life and in the months following her homegoing, heaven's reality struck me. Heaven was the culmination of Mom's salvation and would one day be the culmination of mine. God's presence, experienced to its fullest only in heaven, was the joy of Mom's salvation, and that same joy awaits me.

The Culmination of My Salvation—Heaven

One evening Todd read Psalm 21 to me; and as he read, I replaced the word *king* with *Mom* and the personal pronouns *him* or *his* with *she* or *her*. For the first time since her physical death, I could picture Mom in heaven without tears in my eyes. The joy that picture brought was greater than the sorrows of the good-bye process our family had walked through. I have rewritten this Psalm below with Mom's name in it.

> O Lord, in Your strength Mom rejoices, and in Your
> salvation how greatly she exults! You have given Mom her
> heart's desire, and have not withheld the request of her lips.
> Selah.

> For You meet her with rich blessings; You set a crown of
> fine gold on her head. She asked life of You, You gave it to her,
> length of days forever and ever. Her glory is great through Your
> salvation; splendor and majesty You bestow upon her. For You
> make her most blessed forever; You make her glad with the joy
> of Your presence. For Mom trusts in the LORD, and through
> the lovingkindness of the Most High she will not be moved.
> ~Psalm 21:1–7~

Heaven was the culmination of Mom's salvation; and one day, I will experience the same climatic ending to my salvation story. Mom was and is experiencing the "glory" or glorification stage of her salvation that had been promised when she accepted Christ as her Savior. Her "heart's desire" is being met. Her faith, full founded in "the lovingkindness of the Most High," is now a reality, and she will "not be moved" from her Savior's presence.

The Joy of My Salvation—Jesus

Months after Mom's passing, a painting by Kerolos Safwat circulated social media. This Egyptian artist entitled his piece "First Day in Heaven." It is a picture of a thirty- or forty-year-old woman in the arms of Jesus. It looks like the woman had just run to Jesus and jumped into His arms. There He holds her with her feet off the ground much like a father does when his child races to meet him when he returns home from work. In the painting, Jesus greets her with a huge welcoming hug. The woman's face contains a look of utter joy. One can almost hear her peals of childlike laughter. Her face is carefree, and this is truly the best moment of her life. She has no tears, no fears, no heartaches, or sorrows; nothing is holding her back from complete joy and contentment. This picture brought tears to my eyes. This was and is Mom. This picture encapsulated what she was and is experiencing in the presences of her Creator and Savior. And one day, that would be me in the picture.

All the stories I had heard as a child of the streets of gold, the gates of pearl, the lion and lamb laying down together, and the men and women of Scripture filling the streets made heaven feel more like a fairy tale than a place as real as earth. As I looked at Kerolos Safwat's painting, all those other pictures of heaven faded into the background. Heaven's reality became concrete for me because of the stabilizing truth that heaven is where my Savior lives and waits for my arrival. The One who died in my place and rose to conquer the death I deserved is waiting there for me just like He was eagerly awaiting Mom's arrival. Jesus spoke of His anticipation of His children's homecoming in the book of John. He is in heaven preparing my home for me; and one day, He will call me home.

> Let not your hearts be troubled. Believe in God; believe also in Me. In My Father's house are many rooms. If it were not so, would I have told you that I go to prepare a place for you? And if I go and prepare a place for you, I will come again and will take you to Myself, that where I am you may be also.
> ~John 14:1–3~

The Completeness of Heaven—God's Presence and Blessings

In the months leading up to and following Mom's passing, I was disheartened at how many hymns spoke of death. I dreaded singing these songs. Many of them were set to slow and somber melodies that only added to the sorrow that was threatening to choke out my joy. My mind was full of questions as we sang these songs: *Why did we have to focus on such sadness when there were so many joys here on earth to rejoice in? Why, after facing the heartache of coming death in our family all week long, did I have to sing about it in church on Sunday? Why could I not escape the sadness just for a few moments each week while worshipping with God's people in His house?*

As mentioned earlier, God had begun to open my eyes to my need to spend more time thinking about the humanly "sad" topics of life. As I pondered these topics, I realized that my comfortable American Christian life was incomplete. Paul spoke of the partial nature of life here on earth in 1 Corinthians 13. In the following verses, the word *perfect* can be rendered *complete*.[10]

> But when the perfect comes, the partial will pass away. For now we see in a mirror dimly, but then face to face. Now I now in in part; then I shall know fully, even as I have been fully known.
> ~1 Corinthians 13:10, 12~

There was a reason songwriters of all ages chose death and heaven as the topics of their songs. Life on earth was meant to be incomplete because I have been separated from God's physical presence due to sin in my life and in the world around me. I was created for something that I cannot attain here—a personal relationship with God lived in His physical presence. God has allowed me a taste (the "partial" spoken of in 1 Corinthians 13:10) of the joys of heaven through Scripture and the many blessings He has brought into my life. But the completeness of those joys will only be found in His presence in heaven. As these truths began to take root in my heart, I started to long for the completeness and rest of heaven. God was starting to break down the strong ties that bound me to earthly joys.

Relinquishing of Earthly Ties

The process of Mom's physical death taught me to loosen my grip on the temporary, earthly ties God had blessed me with. In the face of the heart-wrenching symptoms of brain cancer, I started praying that God would take Mom home. I now understood how much better the presence of God was than any of the past life we had experienced as a family.

Mom had a blessed life here on earth. It was not perfect or easy, but I think she would have agreed with the psalmist:

> The Lord is my chosen portion and my cup;
> You hold my lot. The line have fallen for me in
> pleasant places; indeed I have a beautiful inheritance.
> ~Psalm 16:5–6~

I would have and still would echo these words in Psalm 16 to describe my life. I have enjoyed the beauties of creation, the joys of traveling to different countries, the adventures of meeting new people, the comforts of a beautiful home, the love of a godly man, the laughter of friends and family, the opportunity to study for and earn a master's degree, and the kicks of the little baby inside me. My husband has repeatedly said, "Jenn, God has given us a good life." Yes, He has.

Why has God so richly blessed me? God gave me these gifts to remind me of greater joys to come. So often I look at the blessings in my life and fear their removal instead of praising God for them. I must hand these gifts back to God for His safe-keeping. It took the painful end-of-life process Mom experienced to teach me to hold these partial blessings and delights loosely so I would be prepared to one day exchange them for something far better. I have yet to master this process.

In Luke 12 Jesus warned of the covetousness that will prevent me from a biblical view of God's blessings. A rich man took great delight in his earthly blessings, but he allowed those gifts to distract him from God and the blessings waiting for him in heaven. He never took time to ponder how the incomplete gifts of earth point to the completed delights of heaven, to thank God for those gifts, or to ask God what he should do with the earthly joys given to him.

> And He said to them, "Take care, and be on your guard against all covetousness, for one's life does not consist in the abundance of his possessions." And He told them a parable, saying, "The land of a rich man produced plentifully, and he thought to himself, 'What shall I do, for I have nowhere to store my crops?' and he said, 'I will do this: I will tear down my barns and build larger ones, and there I will store all my grain and my goods. And I will say to my soul, "Soul, you have ample goods laid up for many years; relax, eat, drink, be merry."' But God said to him, 'Fool! This night your soul is required of you, and the things you have prepared, whose will they be?' So is the one who lays up treasure for himself and is not rich toward God."
> ~Luke 12:15–21~

This process of holding earthly ties loosely is something I am still learning to do. I am learning to say to Todd, "If we both live that long, then let's do this." I am learning to speak of this little life inside me to others with the phrase, "Lord willing, in November this little one will be in our home." I am learning to pray, "Lord, the joys that so richly surround me on earth are but a foretaste of heaven. When my job here is done, take me home. May I never complain of the means You use to get me there. Teach me to long for heaven while fully enjoying the life You have given me here. You love my husband, my child, and my family more than I do. You can take far better care of them than I can. Teach me to hold my loved ones loosely so I eagerly enter into my journey home when that times comes. Lord, teach me to eagerly let them go home to You when You call them. They will experience joys in heaven far beyond anything they can experience here on this incomplete earth. May I never hold them back from You."

I write these words with tears in my eyes, for I can't imagine life without my siblings, my Dad and his sweet new wife, my husband, my child, or the freedoms given to me here in America. Yet, through Mom's death, God taught me and is still teaching me to hold loosely the incomplete delights of earth so my hands are free to receive and my heart is eager to experience the fullness of joy and rest in His presence in heaven.

It was difficult to watch Mom's end-of-life story unfold, but God used her death to change my perspective of heaven and earth and to deepen my understanding of His amazing plan of salvation. At the end of Mom's life, I had to echo the words of the psalmist:

> Precious in the sight of the Lord is the death of His saints.
> ~Psalm 116:15~

CHAPTER 6
GRACE AND SPACE

As God taught me the spiritual truths I have shared in Chapters 1–5, He also taught me how to practically live out these truths in my interactions with others and in my daily choices. Chapters 6 and 7 cover the practical lessons I learned for the day-to-day valley journey.

Death is full of emotions—the joy of yesterday's memories and last moments spent together, the agony of good-byes and unfulfilled dreams, the uncertainty of the future, the exhaustion of sleepless nights, the weariness of waiting for what is coming while clinging to what is left, and the overwhelming balancing act of the life that continues on with the life that has suddenly come to a halt. These emotions were physically and mentally taxing. I desperately needed God's grace to successfully navigate the emotions of the valley and to purposefully exhibit God's grace in my interactions with others.

Give Grace

There are two kinds of grace displayed in Scripture—the grace God gives me as His child and the grace I must give to others.

God's Grace

God's grace was extended to me when He gave me eternal life through Christ's death and resurrection. Because of God's grace, I am also a recipient of His forgiveness, mercy, goodness, and love. Paul shows the connection between God's grace and these other attributes in Ephesians and Titus. I have added italics in the following verses for emphasis.

> In Him we have redemption through His blood,
> the *forgiveness* of our trespasses, according to the
> riches of His *grace*, which He lavished upon us, in
> all wisdom and insight making known to us the
> mystery of His will, according to His purpose,
> which He set forth in Christ...
> ~Ephesians 1:7–9~

> But God, being rich in *mercy*, because of the
> great *love* with which He loved us, even when
> we were dead in our trespasses, made us alive
> together with Christ—by *grace* you have been
> saved—and raised us up with Him and seated
> us with Him in the heavenly places in Christ
> Jesus, so that in the coming ages He might
> show the immeasurable riches of His *grace*
> in *kindness* toward us in Christ Jesus.
> ~Ephesians 2:4–7~

> But when the *goodness* and *loving kindness*
> of God our Savior appeared, He saved us,
> not because of works done by us in
> righteousness, but according to His own
> *mercy*, by the washing of regeneration and
> renewal of the Holy Spirit, whom He poured
> out on us richly through Jesus Christ our Savior,
> so that being justified by His *grace* we might
> become heirs according to the hope of eternal life.
> ~Titus 3:4–7~

In Psalm 103 David wrote about God's undeserved grace displayed through His forgiveness. David concluded his psalm with two incredible statements. First, he compared God's compassion (or *love* and *mercy*) with that of a father toward his child.[11] Second, he compared himself to dust.

> As a father shows compassion to his
> children, so the LORD shows compassion
> to those who fear Him. For He knows our
> frame; He remembers that we are dust.
> ~Psalm 103:13–14~

In my valley journey I was daily confronted with my own "dustiness" or failures. How desperately I needed God's abundant, never-failing grace! My faith was small, and my fears were great. My patience wore thin, and my joy faltered. I failed to cast my burdens on God, and I doubted God's truth. Yet, God compassionately revealed His grace to me through His immediate forgiveness, mercy, goodness, and love. I realized that if God, who sees my dust-like nature, can exhibit such compassion toward me when I have caused Him great offense, than I needed to show that same compassion to those around me

One Another Grace

In the face of *my* overwhelming weaknesses, God opened my eyes to the hurts of those around me. If I was struggling with my own failings, there was a good chance they were too. If I so desperately needed God's grace to just get through each new day in the valley, then there had to be others who were as overwhelmed as I was. God greatly humbled me as He convicted me of my need to intentionally practice giving grace to others.

As I looked back over my years as a believer, I realized that words I had said or prayed in an attempt to comfort other Christians in their times of crisis were not always helpful or comforting. These phrases included "God works all things together for good," "God can still work miracles," "Praise the Lord, you will see your relative again," and "We weep not as those who have no hope."

In my personal valley journey, these same phrases, now spoken to me in an attempt to comfort, often created more hurt than comfort. In the midst of the emotional turmoil following Mom's diagnosis, these words filled me with fears, doubts, and guilt. The following thoughts raced through my mind when I heard these Christian clichés: *The good that will come from this cancer is that Mom will see God. But I will still be left behind with unfulfilled dreams and prayers answered with a "no." What if God chooses to not miraculously heal Mom here on earth because my faith is so small? If He doesn't heal Mom, what am I supposed to say to these believers? God already performed the miracle in healing Mom's soul on the day of her salvation, and one day, He will heal her body so she will never be sick again. Isn't that the miracle in all this—that Mom will see God and will never deal with pain, sickness, or sin again? Yes, I will see Mom one day, but that is decades away and brings no comfort today as I watch cancer change Mom. Do other believers really think I shouldn't be crying? If I cry gut-wrenching sobs and my eyes are swollen for most of this valley journey, does that mean I am weeping as one who has no hope? Am I disgracing the name of God with constant tears of sadness?*

As these thoughts threatened my peace of mind and heart, I began to learn one of the greatest practical lessons of the valley. Grief affects human communication. My emotions left me vulnerable thus affecting my own interpretation of others' words. During her life Mom often challenged me with a verse from Psalm. God brought this verse to mind many times as I learned to communicate with others during my journey.

> Great peace have those who love Your law;
> nothing can make them stumble.
> ~Psalm 119:165~

The word *stumble* can be translated as *offend*.[12] Psalm 119 reminded me of the value God places on letting peace instead of offense (doubt, guilt, or fear) rule my heart. As I learned to focus on the intentions of those speaking and to humbly admit my failed attempts to comfort others in the past, God allowed His peace to stabilize my emotions and thoughts through the truth of His Word.

Intentions

The ones speaking these words of comfort never intended them to be hurtful. When people are not sure what to say or are deeply hurting, words can come across as unintentionally brash or condemning when they were meant to be encouraging and full of hope. Some people were in as much pain as I was. Their words reflected this pain, and I could not take their words as intended against me. Others were simply trying to offer comfort in the best way they could. Some verses, meant to lift up my weary soul, were spoken out of context or not carefully applied. The speaker had no way of knowing that these verses brought unintentional guilt instead of the intended encouragement (see Tears of Fear and Tears of Hope and Absence in Chapter 3). The same grace God gave me daily when He saw my feeble "dusty" (Psalm 103:14) attempts to give Him glory was exactly what I needed to give to the dear believers who were attempting to comfort to me.

Humility

God had humbled me by revealing my need for His daily grace to just survive this valley journey. I was humbled again as I realized that I was guilty of the same type of communication that was now hurtful to me. I had often tried to comfort others by offering clichés of hope that caused only discouragement. I had quoted Scripture passages or truths to my hurting friends without considering context. I learned (and am still learning) from my own valley experience how to use grace-filled words to encourage others who would walk this pathway after me.

One Another Verses

There were many verses God brought to mind as He instructed me in grace-filled interactions with others during times of crisis. These verses are often referred to as the "one another" verses.

> Be kind to one another, tenderhearted, forgiving
> one another, as God in Christ forgave you.
> ~Ephesians 4:32~

> Let us not become conceited, provoking
> one another, envying one another.
> ~Galatians 5:26~

> Bearing with one another and, if one has a
> complaint against another, forgiving each other; as
> the Lord has forgiven you, so you also must forgive.
> ~Colossians 3:13~

> See that no one repays anyone evil for evil, but always
> seek to do good to one another and to everyone.
> ~1 Thessalonians 5:15~

> Do not speak evil against one another, brothers.
> The one who speaks against a brother or judges
> his brother, speaks evil against the law and judges
> the law. But if you judge the law, you are not
> a doer of the law but a judge.
> ~James 4:11~

> Do not grumble against one another,
> brothers, so that you may not be judged;
> behold, the Judge is standing at the door.
> ~James 5:9~

> Therefore, confess your sins to one another
> and pray for one another, that you may be
> healed. The prayer of a righteous person
> has great power as it is working.
> ~James 5:16~

> Above all, keep loving one another earnestly,
> since love covers a multitude of sins.
> ~I Peter 4:8~

The focus of many of these verses is on the silent heart attitudes of forgiveness, love, and prayer. I began to realize that grace-filled interactions with others often meant the silencing of Jenn's words so that God's Word would be preeminent. God was and always will be a better encourager than I ever could be.

As I recognized the need to silence my own words when attempting to comfort others, I began to realize that the giving of grace is often coupled with the giving of space. In their own valley journeys, believers need space to learn what God was teaching them without my human thoughts or instructions interfering.

Give Space

I have explained that this book is a personal testimony of what God taught me in the valley of the shadow of death (see A Personal Valley). Many others were affected by Mom's cancer. Each one needed space and freedom to grow and learn from God.

Giving space meant that I rid myself of my preconceived ideas of what grief should look like or how someone should respond to a given situation. Giving space meant allowing my loved ones the space to be their own unique person in their grief and allowing God to work in their lives (as He was working in mine).

From my teaching experience, I know the lessons my students remembered the most were the ones they had to learn on their own. I would provide guidance while they learned through the process of discovery. This type of learning environment required humble silence on my part. As my students mentally worked to synthesize the details of the lesson into a main idea, they came to rely on the various gifts and abilities each one of them brought to the lesson. Struggling as a team through the discovery process led to a camaraderie or unity as they reached the conclusion of the lesson.

Family members and a few close friends applied these same principles in their interactions with me during my valley journey. Their humble silence and constant edification solidified our friendship into a partnership that will stand the many trials yet to come.

Humility of Silence

When my students were engaged in a discovery lesson, my silence was key to their success. Silence provided the quiet space they needed to wrestle through the principles and concepts of the lesson as they moved toward their final conclusion.

Just as it took great restraint for me to step down from the lecture podium, it took great humility to be the silent brothers and sisters in Christ who watched me wrestle through Scripture. It took humility to refrain from always confronting, talking, or giving advice. The believers who exhibited this humility of silence practiced the "patience" and "bearing of me in love" that Paul spoke of in Ephesians.

> With all humility and gentleness, with patience,
> bearing with one another in love,…
> ~Ephesians 4:2~

How I needed this forbearance from others during my valley journey. I had no clue how weak I was until I faced the reality of Mom's upcoming death. Anxiety attacks, sleepless nights, doubts of the basic tenets of my faith, and endless weariness of soul drained me of all my resources, answers, and confidence. In these vulnerable moments, I was grateful for the wise believers who knew how to effectively use God's Word to pray for and encourage me without overwhelming me with man's words.

When I hesitantly shared my struggles with a few individuals, I expected a well-rehearsed lecture (thus my great hesitation to open up). Instead their responses were full of quiet acceptance, understanding, and encouragement. They responded with humility as they acknowledged their own similar struggles in past situations. Some of them shared a verse that God had used to grow their own faith. Then they grew silent.

I realized later their silence was not because they lacked spiritual wisdom. It was an indication of their humility. They understood from experience that part of the value of the lesson was what I gained through my own wrestling with Scripture. By stepping back verbally, they gave me space to discover the principles and concepts that would eventually lead to the answers found only in God's Word. Paul spoke of the need for each believer be fully educated in God's Word.

> So that Christ may dwell in your hearts through
> faith—that you, being rooted and grounded in love,
> may have strength to comprehend with all the saints
> what is the breadth and length and height and depth,
> and to know the love of Christ that surpasses knowledge,
> that you may be filled with all the fullness of God.
> ~Ephesians 3:17–19~

> Do your best to present yourself to God as one
> approved, a worker who has no need to be
> ashamed, rightly handling the word of truth.
> ~2 Timothy 2:15~

One example of how the humility of silence gave me space to grow in my faith came from one of my sisters. I shared earlier in Chapter 4 that I found myself doubting whether what I had believed my whole life concerning Jesus and the plan of salvation was true. I finally opened up to one of my sisters about this struggle. Her response was simple, "Jenn, I think most people facing death have similar doubts." She acknowledged the reality of my struggle and humbly backed off. She did not set forth a three-point outline. She did not belittle my fears with judgment for such a lack of faith. She prayed for me and gave me the space to work through the season of doubt with the only source that would answer all my questions—God's Word. Her humility was seen in the fact she did not intervene with her own well-crafted words, instead she prayed and allowed God to work.

As is true in a well-run discovery lesson, believers who were trained in silent humility also knew how to use their own strengths and the strengths of those around them to create an effective learning environment in times of difficulty.

Continual Edification

As a teacher, I found that each student brought his own unique strengths to a discovery lesson. In the groups that experienced success, the participants focused on each other's strengths and not their weaknesses. In fact, many times, one student's strength compensated for another student's weakness, which allowed more learning for all.

In the same way, each person going through the valley of the shadow of Mom's death brought his or her own unique set of strengths to the journey. As we humbly focused on each other's strengths, the weaknesses of each person were no longer hindrances to growth. Instead the strengths and weakness of each person became opportunities for edification.

One example of edification took place in my church auditorium on a Sunday morning. I walked into the sanctuary and was greeted by one of the ushers. He shook my hand and, in his quiet way, thanked me for my continual smile and spirit of joy. My eyes brimmed with unexpected tears. I had often wondered if I was an encouragement to anyone during my journey through the valley of the shadow of death. My emotions were so intense, and the hurt was so deep. Life-changing decisions were coming at me with lightning speed, and my own inadequacies and sinful responses were never far out of my spiritual view. This older saint was within his biblical rights to approach me at any time with a fatherly tone and gentle spirit and rebuke me for a hundred different actions, thoughts, doubts, fears, and decisions I should have handled differently. Instead he took a quiet moment to simply point out a strength of mine that was an encouragement to him. I have clung to his words to this day. It was as though time stood still while he held my hand, looked me in the eyes, and lifted up my tired soul with a simple "thank you." This man was a living example of edification.

The words *edification* or *edify* convey the idea of building up another's faith.[13] Through the examples of others, I learned that one of the best ways to exhibit grace during emotionally charged moments was to build up those around me. This edification happened when I used my own strengths to encourage others or as I pointed out their strengths that offset my weaknesses.

Let me share how others edified me during my darkest days.

My faith was built up when family members and friends shared in my emotions.

> Rejoice with those who rejoice,
> weep with those who weep.
> ~Romans 12:15~

My faith was built up when others encouraged me by knowing what would lift my spirits the most (a verse of Scripture, a text, a coffee, a gift card for fast food, or a night out with friends).

> Therefore encourage one another and
> build one another up, just as you are doing.
> ~1 Thessalonians 5:11~

My faith was built up when my sister or a friend shared a song or verse with a unique promise I could claim that day.

> And do not get drunk with wine, for that
> is debauchery, but be filled with the Spirit,
> addressing one another in psalms and hymns
> and spiritual songs, singing and making melody
> to the Lord with your heart,…
> ~Ephesians 5:18–19~

> And now I commend you to God and to the
> word of His grace, which is able to build you
> up and to give you the inheritance among
> all those who are sanctified.
> ~Acts 20:32~

My faith was built up by the prayers of many individuals who daily brought our family before God's throne of grace.

> Praying at all times in the Spirit, with all prayer
> and supplication. To that end, keep alert with
> all perseverance, making supplication for all
> the saints,…
> ~Ephesians 6:18~

My faith was built up when others laughed with me.

> A joyful heart is good medicine, but
> a crushed spirit dries up the bones.
> ~Proverbs 17:22~

My faith was built up when friends found creative ways to do something kind for our family (an unexpected Thanksgiving meal, a paid-in-full family photo shoot, and a weekly meal for my parents).

> And let us not grow weary of doing good,
> for in due season we will reap, if we do not
> give up. So then, as we have opportunity,
> let us do good to everyone, and especially
> to those who are of the household of faith.
> ~Galatians 6:9–10~

The edification of my faith by other believers during my valley journey resulted in a unity that will stand the test of time.

Unity of the Spirit

When I gave my students the space to work through the many problems that arose on the pathway to discovery and as they learned to set each other up for greater learning potential by utilizing each other's strengths, they eventually reached the "ah-ha" moment of the lesson. As the main idea of the lesson became clear in their minds, their natural response was a show of solidarity. There was a sudden exclamation of understanding followed by a flurry of words as they each verbalized the lesson in their own way. The high fives, smiles of satisfaction, shouts of success, and slaps on the back were shared by all. They had silently worked through their struggles, helped each other compensate for individual weaknesses, and now they stood unified as a confident group of eager learners at the finish line of discovery.

One this side of my journey, I find myself standing in a safety net of unity. Both those who patiently stood by me in silence as I struggled to understand the lessons of the valley and those who continually built me up using their strengths and faithfully pointing out my strengths now surround me as faithful partners in this ever-changing journey of life. We do not face future struggles alone. We gave each other the grace and space to hurt, to confess our sins to each other, to pray for each other, and to humbly accept help from one another. United we stand stronger than we were alone. No wonder God desires this strength of unity among His children.

> If possible, so far as it depends on
> you, live peaceably with all.
> ~Romans 12:18~

> Behold, how good and pleasant it
> is when brothers dwell in unity!
> ~Psalm 133:1~

> I appeal to you, brothers, by the name of
> our Lord Jesus Christ, that all of you agree,
> and that there be no divisions among you,
> but that you be united in the same mind
> and the same judgment.
> ~1 Corinthians 1:10~

> Bearing with one another and, if one
> has a complaint against another, forgiving each
> other; as the Lord has forgiven you, so you
> also must forgive. And above all these put
> on love, which binds everything together
> in perfect harmony.
> ~Colossians 3:13–14~

Love One Another

As I wrote this chapter, my mind kept going back to 1 Corinthians 13. Paul used the term *love* to describe the principle of grace and space. He outlined love in the following way:

The need for love: (vv. 1–3)

> If I speak in the tongues of men and of angels,
> but have not love, I am a noisy gong or a
> clanging cymbal. And if I have prophetic
> powers, and understand all mysteries and all
> knowledge, and if I have all faith, so as to
> remove mountains, but have not love, I
> am nothing. If I give away all I have, and
> if I deliver up my body to be burned, but
> have not love, I gain nothing.

The actions of love: (vv. 4–7)

> Love is patient and kind; does not envy
> or boast; it is not arrogant or rude. It does
> not insist on its own way; it is not irritable or
> resentful; it does not rejoice at wrong doing,
> but rejoices with the truth. Love bears all
> things, believes all things, hopes
> all things, endures all things.

The unending nature of love: (v. 8)

> Love never ends. As for prophecies, they
> will pass away; as for tongues, they will
> cease; as for knowledge, it will pass away.

The unity of love: (vv. 9–12)

> For we know in part and we prophesy in part, but when the perfect comes, the partial will pass away. When I was a child, I spoke like a child, I thought like a child, I reasoned like a child. When I became a man, I gave up childish ways. For now we see in a mirror dimly, but then face to face. Now I know in part; then I shall know fully, even as I have been fully known.

The superiority of love: (v. 13)

> So now faith, hope, and love abide, these three; but the greatest of these is love.

Oh, that I would love others the same way God has loved me as I practice the principle of grace and space in my interactions with those who walk through the valley of the shadow of death. May I never forget the importance Jesus placed on biblical love.

> By this all people will know that you are
> My disciples, if you have love for one another.
> ~John 13:35~

CHAPTER 7
THE DAY-TO-DAY
JOURNEY

The lesson of grace and space was vitally important to my social interactions during my valley journey. The lessons I'll share with you in this chapter were necessary for my personal survival in the day-by-day journey through the valley of the shadow of death. These lessons made the journey less overwhelming.

Appreciate the Normal

In the first few weeks of my valley journey, a wise friend informed me that I would find myself unable to relate to people as I walked through the valley. I thought he was crazy. I had always been a sociable person. I could not imagine being unable to relate to others. But the day came when I realized he was right. Life was changing so quickly I had a hard time adjusting, and this became apparent in social situations.

My friend understood that I had started a journey of "the new normal." Normal was forever changing in the valley of the shadow. As I encountered the unpredictable life inside the valley, I craved the predictable live I had always known.

During this time I loved hearing about my friends' normal life experiences. Hearing these stories gave me a chance to recover from the most recent season of tears while I focused on someone else.

I also learned to enjoy the routine elements of everyday life. I took time to enjoy the sunshine while I drove to work, to smile at the inevitably crazy antics of my junior high students, and to find relief in the time limits set by the rising and setting sun and changing seasons of the year. I gained a new appreciation for God's orderliness in creation and His goodness in giving me work to perform each day.

> To Him who made the great lights, for His steadfast love endures forever; the sun to rule over the day, for His steadfast love endures forever; the moon and stars to rule over the night, for His steadfast love endures forever;…
> ~Psalm 136:7–9~

> Yours is the day, Yours also the night; You have established the heavenly lights and the sun. You have fixed all the boundaries of the earth; You have made summer and winter.
> ~Psalm 74:16–17~

> For everything there is a season, and a time for every matter under heaven: a time to be born, and a time to die; a time to plant, and a time to pluck up what is planted; a time to kill, and a time to heal; a time to break down, and a time to build up; a time to weep, and a time to laugh; a time to mourn, and a time to dance; a time to cast away stones, and a time to gather stones together; a time to embrace, and a time to refrain from embracing; a time to seek, and a time to lose; a time to keep, and a time to cast away; a time to tear, and a time to sew; a time to keep silence, and a time to speak; a time to love, and a time to hate; a time for war, and a time for peace.
> ~Ecclesiastes 3:1–8~

> The Lord God took the man and put him in the garden of Eden to work it and keep it.
> ~Genesis 2:15~

> In all toil there is profit, but mere talk tends only to poverty.
> ~Proverbs 14:23~

Value the Gift of Laughter

> A joyful heart is good medicine, but
> a crushed spirit dries up the bones.
> ~Proverbs 17:22~

My parents raised five children who all have a healthy sense of humor. Dad and Mom never let us take ourselves too seriously. Laughter was a part of our lives growing up. We would laugh over meals that had gone horribly wrong because of missing ingredients. We would laugh at Dad and the boys as they sang karaoke. We would laugh as we secretly planned water fights or tried to tag each other during our wiffle ball games. We would laugh as we sang some of our favorite family songs or when Dad would use his goofy voices on long road trips. We grew up loving to laugh.

Amid the heart-breaking emotions I shared in Chapters 3 and 6, what a relief laughter brought to our family during our valley journey. Let me share two examples of how humor lightened the mood during highly emotional moments.

All Together

During one of Mom's hospital visits that had been particular heart-wrenching, we all gathered around her hospital bed. Mom was alert and clearly enjoying the fact that everyone was together. One of the siblings spoke up at some point in the conversation, "Hey, Mom, if you really wanted us all together, you didn't need to get a brain tumor. You could have just asked us to come see you."

A Two-for-One Special

On January 19, 2016, Mom underwent a three-plus hour long brain tumor resection. Everyone's nerves were wound pretty tight. We gathered in the waiting room doing our best to stay preoccupied. As one can imagine, Dad had a lot on his mind. At one point he said something that made all of us kids scratch our heads in bewilderment. He realized what he had said, rolled his eyes, and made some comment about his own brain. One of my siblings piped up "Dad, maybe they have a two-for-one special on brain surgeries today! Let's ask!"

Yes, laughter was and is an incredibly good and needed medicine in the valley of the shadow. By the day of Mom's funeral, my family could laugh and cry in the same sentence without thinking twice about it. I am so grateful for my parents' emphasis on clean humor and laughter. Many times laughter was the one thing that made the darkest days survivable.

Prioritize

Different seasons of life have required me to re-prioritize essentials and non-essentials in my life. Activities that were once essentials before my valley (i.e., attending most church activities, setting aside time each week with friends) immediately became nonessentials when I entered the valley. This re-prioritizing allowed me the times of silence that were needed as I wrestled through the lessons God was teaching me. When God led me into a different season of life after Mom's passing, my list of essentials and nonessentials changed again

Take the Time

It took time to grieve. It took time to learn the next lesson God would teach in the silence that followed gut-wrenching grief. This season in the valley of the shadow required time I did not always want to give, but I had much to learn about sitting still (Psalm 46:10). I was confronted with this need early on in my valley journey. Below are some thoughts I posted online on December 27, 2015, three days after we were told Mom had a tumor.

> I would love to "shortcut" or rush through this season of life—the sleepless nights, tears, and physical ache of it.
>
> But if I rush through this season, will some eternal calamity happen in someone else's life? Will someone not hear the gospel (a doctor or nurse) because I was selfish and don't want to walk this path? God gives such great value to souls that He died for them. Why can I not simply walk this journey in hopes of winning some to their Savior?
>
> If I rush along this path, will I be in danger spiritually? Yes, I know I will be. There are many lessons of God's great care and love that are learned only in the valley. If I rush this journey, I will miss out on seeing God's deliverance (Psalm 34:7). I will also miss out on the many good things my Shepherd desires to teach me (Psalm 34:10). Yes, to "shortcut" this path would be a calamity for my character.
>
> So though I desperately want to wake up and find this all to be a bad dream or to escape into a different world, God says "Be still and know that I am God…" (Psalm 46:10).

I have always and will always have the tendency to want to rush through difficult days. I still echo the words of Psalm 46:10 in my prayers. "Lord, teach me to be still and know that You are God."

I am so thankful God patiently taught me the valuable and practical lessons of appreciating normal life, valuing laughter, prioritizing essentials and nonessentials, and slowing down in the valley of the shadow. These four day-to-day practices brought simplicity to overwhelming days and order to the upheaval that threatened my stability.

As God walked with me through the valley of the shadow, He forced me deeper into His Word as He taught me spiritual and practical lessons that would guide me through the remainder of my life. His patient care of me was evident every day. And now I can truly say, "Lord, thank You, for taking me through the valley of the shadow of death."

CONCLUSION

The valley of the shadow of death has held the sweetest lessons of my life thus far. My gentle, loving Guide never left my side. After months of tears and wrestling, the far side of the valley came into view. God convicted me of the need to write down what He had taught me so I would never forget the beauty of Who He is and the value of what He teaches in the darkest days.

Because of this journey, I better understand and appreciate the psalmist's words, "It is good for me that I was afflicted, that I might learn Your statutes" (Psalm 119:71).

APPENDIX
WHAT IS A BIBLE-BELIEVING CHRISTIAN?

As a Bible-believing Christian, I believe that God's Word is the ultimate source of truth. Within its pages, the Bible reveals who God is and His plan for the human race and for you. God's plan for you is explained below in seven truth statements from God's Word.

Truth 1: You were created for the glory of God and for a personal relationship with God as His child.

> For by Him all things were created, in heaven and on earth, visible and invisible, whether thrones or dominions or rulers or authorities—all things were created through Him and for Him. And He is before all things, and in Him all things hold together.
> ~Colossians 1:16–17~

> And this is eternal life, that they know You, the only true God, and Jesus Christ whom You have sent.
> ~John 17:3~

Truth 2: Sin in your life (not loving God with your whole being and not loving others as you love yourself) has kept you from glorifying God and enjoying a personal relationship with God.

> For all have sinned and fall short of the glory of God[.]
> ~Romans 3:23~

> But your iniquities have made a separation between you and your God, and your sins have hidden His face from you so that He does not hear.
> ~Isaiah 59:2~

Truth 3: The consequence of sin is death (physical and spiritual separation from God for eternity).

> For the wages of sin is death, but the free gift
> of God is eternal life in Christ Jesus our Lord.
> ~Romans 6:23~

Truth 4: Because of His love for you, Jesus Christ (God's Son), took the punishment for your sins by dying on the cross. God brought Jesus back to life, proving His power over sin and death.

> But God shows His love for us in that while
> we were still sinners, Christ died for us.
> ~Romans 5:8~

> For God so loved the world, that He gave
> His only Son, that whoever believes in Him
> should not perish but have eternal life.
> ~John 3:16~

> For I delivered to you as of first importance
> what I also received: that Christ died for our
> sins in accordance with the Scriptures, that
> He was buried, that He was raised on the
> third day in accordance with the Scriptures[.]
> ~1 Corinthians 15:3–4~

Truth 5: By trusting (depending) on Jesus and His work on the cross and repenting (turning away) from your sin, you are welcomed into God's family as His child. The glory of God and the personal relationship with God that you were created for are now a reality.

> For by grace you have been saved through faith.
> And this is not your own doing; it is the gift of God,
> not a result of works, so that no one may boast.
> ~Ephesians 2:8–9~

> No, I tell you; but unless you repent,
> you will all likewise perish.
> ~Luke 13:3~

> And how you turned to God from idols
> to serve the living and true God[.]
> ~1 Thessalonians 1:9~

> Because, if you confess with your mouth
> that Jesus is Lord and believe in your heart
> that God raised Him from the dead, you
> will be saved. For with the heart one believes
> and is justified, and with the mouth one
> confesses and is saved.
> ~Romans 10:9–10~

> But to all who did receive Him, who believed
> in His name, He gave the right to become
> children of God[.]
> ~John 1:12~

Truth 6: God will keep His promise to save you and welcome you home to heaven as His child.

> For everyone who calls on the name of
> the Lord will be saved.
> ~Romans 10:13~

> Consequently, He is able to save to the uttermost
> those who draw near to God through Him, since
> He always lives to make intercession for them.
> ~Hebrews 7:25~

> In My Father's house are many rooms. If it were
> not so, would I have told you that I go to prepare
> a place for you? And if I go and prepare a place
> for you, I will come again and will take you
> to Myself, that where I am you may be also.
> ~John 14:2–3~

Truth 7: You have the rest of your earthly life to learn about God through His Word. You are not perfect; but as a child of God, you simply ask God for His forgiveness when you sin. He will forgive you.

> Sanctify them in the truth;
> Your word is truth.
> ~John 17:17~

> Indeed, I count everything as loss because
> of the surpassing worth of knowing Christ
> Jesus my Lord. For His sake I have suffered
> the loss of all things and count them as rubbish,
> in order that I may gain Christ.
> ~Philippians 3:8~

> Do not be conformed to this world, but be
> transformed by the renewal of your mind, that
> by testing you may discern what is the will
> of God, what is good and acceptable and perfect.
> ~Romans 12:2~

> If we confess our sins, He is faithful and
> just to forgive us our sins and to cleanse
> us from all unrighteousness.
> ~1 John 1:9~

If you embrace these truths and are willing to live by them, welcome to God's family. I am thrilled to call you my brother or sister in Jesus Christ. If you have questions about these truths or the process of believing these truths, please feel free to contact me at jenn@townsend.me.

ENDNOTES

1. *humble / afflicted*: Strong, James, *Strong's Exhaustive Concordance of the Bible*, Updated Edition (Peabody: Hendrickson Publishers, Inc., 2007), 502, 90

2. *perfect / full age*: ibid., 784, 71

3. *delivered / preserved*: ibid., 253, 80; *saved / preserved*: ibid., 880, 53

4. *saves / helps*: ibid., 880, 53

5. *Baca / weeping*: ibid., 95, 21

6. MacArthur, John, *The MacArthur Study Bible* (Wheaton: Crossway, 2010), 1799, 1800

7. Wiersbe, Warren W., *The Wiersbe Bible Commentary*, 2nd Edition (Colorado Springs: David C. Cook Distribution, 2007), 34

8. *humble / afflicted*: Strong, James, *Strong's Exhaustive Concordance of the Bible*, Updated Edition (Peabody: Hendrickson Publishers, Inc., 2007), 502, 90

9. *LORD / Self-Existent, Eternal God*: ibid., 626, 47

10. *perfect / complete*: ibid., 784, 71

11. *compassion / love* or *mercy*: ibid., 792, 108

12. *stumble / offended*: ibid., 736, 66

13. *edification / building*: ibid., 296, 51; *edify / build*: ibid, 296, 51

Made in the USA
Monee, IL
08 December 2021